Parenting Through Your Patterns

A Schema Therapy Approach to Healing Generational Trauma and Raising Emotionally Resilient Children

Janet Zufan Rose

ISBN: 978-1-7641941-6-7

Isohan Publishing

Table of Contents

Introduction: The Day I Realized I Was Becoming My Mother

The words erupted from my mouth before I could stop them—sharp, cutting, and painfully familiar. "What's wrong with you? Can't you do anything right?" My seven-year-old daughter stood frozen in the kitchen, milk spreading across the floor from the glass she'd dropped. But it wasn't her face I saw in that moment. It was my own, thirty years earlier, standing in a different kitchen with the same terror in my eyes.

My mother's voice had found its way through three decades and out of my mouth.

I dropped to my knees—not to clean the spill, but to pull my daughter close. "I'm sorry," I whispered into her hair. "That wasn't about you. That was never about you." In that moment of painful clarity, I understood something that would change not just my parenting, but my entire understanding of how emotional patterns pass from one generation to the next.

This book exists because of that moment—and because of the thousands of parents I've worked with who've had similar awakenings. Parents who've done the work, read the books about healing from their own childhoods, yet find themselves unconsciously repeating the very patterns they swore they'd never pass on.

What Are Schemas and Why They Matter for Parents

Let me explain schemas in the simplest way possible. Think of them as emotional blueprints laid down in childhood—deep patterns of thinking, feeling, and behaving that shape how we see ourselves and the world. These aren't just thoughts or beliefs; they're entire operating systems that run in the background of our lives, especially when we're stressed, tired, or triggered.

1

Schemas develop when our core emotional needs aren't met consistently in childhood. A child who experiences abandonment develops an abandonment schema—a deep expectation that people they love will leave. A child who grows up without emotional warmth develops an emotional deprivation schema—a belief that their emotional needs won't be met by others.

Here's what makes schemas so powerful in parenting: they operate outside our conscious awareness. You can logically know you're a good parent, that your child is safe and loved, but when your four-year-old says "I hate you" during a tantrum, your abandonment schema might hijack your nervous system. Suddenly, you're not responding to a normal developmental moment—you're reacting to a perceived catastrophic loss.

The research on schemas and intergenerational transmission is clear and sobering. Studies show that parents' unresolved schemas significantly predict their children's emotional and behavioral difficulties. When we parent from our schemas rather than from our wisdom, we inadvertently create the conditions for our children to develop similar patterns.

But here's the hope that fills every page of this book: awareness changes everything. Once you can recognize your schemas in action, you gain the power to pause, breathe, and choose a different response. You become the parent who breaks the cycle.

The Journey from "Adult Children" Books to Active Parenting

Many of you have already walked part of this path. You've read "Adult Children of Emotionally Immature Parents" or similar books. You've done therapy, journaling, maybe even EMDR or other trauma work. You understand your past and how it shaped you. You've grieved, raged, and maybe even forgiven.

But now you're facing a different challenge. It's one thing to understand why you struggle with trust because your father was unpredictable. It's another thing entirely when your toddler's normal testing behavior triggers that old mistrust, and you find yourself seeing manipulation where there's only age-appropriate boundary pushing.

The transition from healing your own wounds to actively parenting while still healing is like learning to dance while building the dance floor. You're simultaneously:

- Managing your own triggers while teaching emotional regulation
- Healing your inner child while raising actual children
- Breaking patterns you're still discovering
- Creating new family dynamics without a healthy model to follow

This book bridges that gap. It's not another book about understanding your childhood—it's about using that understanding to create a different childhood for your own children.

How This Book Works: Healing Yourself While Raising Healthy Children

This isn't a book you read once and put on the shelf. Think of it as a working manual for schema-informed parenting. Each chapter focuses on one of the five core schemas that most commonly affect parenting, but more importantly, each chapter provides:

1. **Recognition tools** - How to spot when your schema is activated
2. **In-the-moment strategies** - What to do when you're triggered

3. **Repair protocols** - How to heal ruptures with your children
4. **Prevention practices** - Daily habits that build resilience
5. **Child-focused techniques** - Age-appropriate ways to meet your children's needs

The magic happens in the integration. As you learn to recognize and soothe your own schemas, you simultaneously create conditions that prevent those same schemas from developing in your children. You become what I call a "cycle-breaker parent"—someone who consciously transforms pain into wisdom, wounds into awareness, patterns into choices.

The Five Core Schemas That Shape Parenting

Through my work with hundreds of families, five schemas consistently emerge as the most impactful on parenting:

1. Abandonment Schema When you carry this schema, separation feels like death. Your child's growing independence triggers primal fear. You might become overprotective, struggle with boundaries, or paradoxically push your child away before they can "leave" you. Your parenting swings between clinging and distancing, creating the very instability you fear.

2. Mistrust Schema
This schema makes you see danger everywhere. Other adults become potential threats. Your child's normal behaviors get interpreted through a lens of suspicion. You might interrogate your child about their day, create walls between your family and the world, or teach hypervigilance instead of healthy caution.

3. Emotional Deprivation Schema Growing up without emotional nurturing leaves you unsure how to provide it. You might meet all your child's physical needs while missing their emotional ones. Feelings become foreign territory—both your child's and your own. You love deeply but struggle to express it in ways your child can receive.

4. Defectiveness Schema This schema whispers that something is fundamentally wrong with you—and by extension, your child. Normal childhood mistakes become evidence of failure. You might become hypercritical, perfectionistic, or swing between harsh judgment and guilty overindulgence. Shame becomes the family language.

5. Failure Schema When you believe you're destined to fail, parenting feels like a test you're constantly failing. Your child's struggles become proof of your inadequacy. You might hover anxiously, doing too much for your child, or withdraw in defeat. Either way, your child doesn't learn they can succeed through their own efforts.

The Promise of This Book: You Can Break the Cycle

Let me be absolutely clear about something: you don't need to be fully healed to be a good parent. Perfect parents don't exist, and if they did, they'd probably raise anxious children who couldn't handle imperfection. What you need is awareness, tools, and the courage to do things differently.

Breaking generational cycles isn't about perfection—it's about progress. It's about catching yourself before you say the words that wounded you. It's about repairing quickly when you mess up. It's about giving your children what you needed and didn't get, even when you're still learning to give it to yourself.

The parents I've worked with have taught me that transformation is possible at any stage. I've seen:

- Parents with severe abandonment schemas raise securely attached children

5

- Parents with mistrust schemas build communities of support
- Parents with emotional deprivation schemas become emotional coaches
- Parents with defectiveness schemas model healthy self-compassion
- Parents with failure schemas celebrate effort over outcome

These parents aren't special or extraordinary. They're simply aware and committed. They've decided that the cycle stops with them.

Case Study Theme: Brief Vignettes of Five Different Parents Recognizing Their Patterns

Maria's Moment - Abandonment Schema Maria's chest tightened as her eight-year-old daughter announced she wanted to sleep at her best friend's house. "It's just one night," her daughter pleaded. But Maria heard her own eight-year-old voice, begging her mother not to leave for another business trip. The schema whispered: "If she can be happy without you, she doesn't need you. If she doesn't need you, she'll leave." Maria recognized the familiar panic and took a breath. This wasn't about being left—it was about her daughter growing up.

James's Awakening - Mistrust Schema "Did anyone talk to you today? What did they say? Why did they say that?" James heard himself interrogating his son after school and suddenly saw his father's suspicious face. Every question his dad had asked carried an accusation, a search for betrayal. James realized he was scanning for dangers that existed in his past, not his son's present. His hypervigilance was creating the very anxiety he wanted to protect against.

Linda's Recognition - Emotional Deprivation Schema Linda sat stiffly as her daughter sobbed about a friendship problem.

She'd bought her daughter new clothes, arranged playdates, done everything "right." But she couldn't find the words of comfort, couldn't offer the emotional presence her daughter craved. In that moment, Linda felt herself as a child, crying alone while her mother efficiently managed the house. She'd learned to provide everything but emotional connection.

Robert's Realization - Defectiveness Schema "You're so stupid! How could you forget your homework again?" The words hung in the air as Robert saw his son's face crumble. It was his father's voice, the one that had convinced him he was fundamentally flawed. Now he was passing that toxic shame to his own son, creating another generation of "never good enough." The cycle was so clear, so painful, so stoppable—if he could find another way.

Sarah's Insight - Failure Schema Sarah watched her daughter struggle with math homework and felt the familiar urge to take over. "Here, let me do it" almost escaped her lips—the same words that had taught her she wasn't capable. Her parents had rescued her from every challenge, confirming her belief that she couldn't succeed alone. Now she was about to steal her daughter's chance to struggle, learn, and grow. The pattern was right there, waiting to be broken.

Practical Elements

Schema Identification Quiz (Quick Version)

Rate each statement from 1 (never true) to 5 (always true):

Abandonment Indicators:

- I panic when my child prefers someone else
- I feel devastated when my child pushes me away
- I worry constantly about losing my child's love
- I have trouble letting my child be independent

- I fear my child will abandon me when they grow up

Mistrust Indicators:

- I question my child extensively about their day
- I'm suspicious of other adults around my child
- I look for signs my child is hiding something
- I have trouble trusting teachers/caregivers
- I see potential harm in normal situations

Emotional Deprivation Indicators:

- I freeze when my child needs emotional comfort
- I focus on practical solutions rather than feelings
- I feel uncomfortable with emotional expressions
- I don't know how to respond to my child's emotions
- I provide things instead of emotional presence

Defectiveness Indicators:

- I'm highly critical of my child's mistakes
- I feel shame when my child misbehaves publicly
- I worry something is "wrong" with my child
- I compare my child negatively to others
- I hear my critical parent's voice in my head

Failure Indicators:

- I do tasks my child could do themselves
- I panic when my child struggles
- I measure my worth by my child's achievements
- I fear my child will fail like I did
- I hover anxiously or withdraw in defeat

"Where You Are Now" Baseline Assessment

For each area, write a brief reflection:

1. **Your Parenting Triggers**: What moments with your child trigger the strongest emotional reactions?
2. **Your Default Responses**: When triggered, what do you typically say or do?
3. **Your Childhood Echoes**: What similarities do you notice between your reactions and your parents'?
4. **Your Children's Responses**: How do your children typically react to your triggered state?
5. **Your Repair Attempts**: How do you currently try to fix things after difficult moments?

Family Pattern Mapping Exercise

Create a three-generation map:

Generation 1 (Your Parents):

- What were their primary parenting patterns?
- What emotional needs went unmet?
- What phrases/behaviors stick in your memory?

Generation 2 (You):

- Which patterns are you repeating?
- Which patterns have you already changed?
- What triggers the old patterns?

Generation 3 (Your Children):

- What patterns might be emerging?
- What different experiences are you providing?
- Where do you see hope for change?

Your Journey Starts Now

This book won't give you a perfect parenting formula because one doesn't exist. What it will give you is awareness—the ability to catch yourself in schema-driven moments and choose differently. It will give you tools—practical strategies for when you're triggered, tired, or overwhelmed. Most importantly, it will give you hope—evidence-based proof that cycles can be broken, that patterns can change, that the pain stops here.

You've already taken the hardest step by picking up this book. You've acknowledged that something needs to change and that you're willing to be the one who changes it. That takes tremendous courage. The parents who've walked this path before you want you to know: it's worth it. Every moment of awareness, every different choice, every repaired rupture moves your family toward healing.

Your children don't need perfect parents. They need aware parents—parents who can see their own patterns, name them, and work to transform them. They need parents who can say, "I'm working on this. This is my stuff, not yours. You are not responsible for my emotions."

The generational healing starts now, with you, in this moment. Let's begin.

Key Takeaways

- **Schemas are emotional blueprints** from childhood that unconsciously drive our parenting behaviors, especially when we're triggered or stressed
- **Five core schemas** most commonly affect parenting: abandonment, mistrust, emotional deprivation, defectiveness, and failure
- **You don't need to be fully healed** to be a good parent— you need awareness, tools, and commitment to doing things differently
- **Breaking cycles happens in small moments** of recognition, pause, and choosing a different response than what was modeled for you

- **Schema-informed parenting** simultaneously heals your wounds while preventing similar patterns from developing in your children
- **Awareness is your superpower**—once you can recognize your schemas in action, you gain the ability to respond rather than react

Chapter 1: When Love Feels Like Leaving - The Abandonment Schema

"If You Really Loved Me, You'd Never Go"

Sarah's hands trembled as she watched her eight-year-old daughter pack her overnight bag. Just a toothbrush, pajamas, and her favorite stuffed elephant. Such simple items, yet each one felt like a small betrayal. "Are you sure you want to go?" Sarah asked for the fourth time. "I could make your favorite pancakes in the morning. We could have a movie night instead."

Her daughter looked up with those earnest brown eyes—her father's eyes, Sarah couldn't help but think. Her father who'd died when Sarah was exactly her daughter's age. "Mom, it's just one night at Emma's house. I'll be back tomorrow."

Just one night. Just like her father had said he'd just be gone for one business trip. Sarah's chest tightened. Logic told her this was different. Her daughter wasn't dying. She was growing up. But her nervous system couldn't tell the difference between healthy separation and catastrophic loss[1].

How Abandonment Fears Create Anxious, Clingy Parenting

The abandonment schema operates like an internal alarm system set to maximum sensitivity. Where others see normal comings and goings, you see potential devastation. Your child's natural drive for independence registers as rejection. Their excitement about new relationships feels like replacement.

This hypervigilance creates a paradox. The more you fear losing your child's love, the more likely you are to drive them away through suffocating behaviors. You become the parent who:

- Texts constantly when your child is with others
- Feels personally rejected when your child prefers friends
- Creates guilt around normal separation ("I guess I'll just eat dinner alone")
- Panic when your child expresses anger or frustration toward you
- Interpret developmental independence as abandonment

The irony cuts deep. Your abandonment schema makes you act in ways that could actually create distance in your relationship. Your child learns that their independence hurts you, that their emotions are dangerous, that they're responsible for your wellbeing. This emotional burden can lead them to either comply and lose themselves, or rebel and create the distance you feared.

Research on attachment shows that children need what's called a "secure base"—a parent who provides both connection and support for exploration[2]. When abandonment fears dominate your parenting, you provide intense connection but block exploration. Your child gets half of what they need, creating their own future struggles with relationships.

The Difference Between Healthy Attachment and Enmeshment

Healthy attachment looks like a dance. You come together, you move apart, you come together again. There's rhythm, flow, and mutual enjoyment. Your child feels safe to explore because they know you'll be there when they return. You feel secure in their love even when they're focused elsewhere.

Enmeshment, on the other hand, feels like being tied together with invisible rope. There's no space to breathe, no room to be separate people. Every movement apart creates pain and panic. In enmeshed families:

- Children's emotions are treated as emergencies
- Parents need constant reassurance of being loved/needed
- Independence is seen as betrayal
- Family loyalty means having no boundaries
- Children become responsible for parent's emotional state

Here's a practical way to tell the difference. Healthy attachment says, "I love you and I want you to have your own experiences." Enmeshment says, "I love you so you can't have experiences without me." One creates security, the other creates anxiety.

Why Some Parents Can't Let Their Children Individuate

Marcus sat in his car outside his son's basketball practice, fighting the urge to leave. Not just leave the parking lot—leave entirely. His sixteen-year-old son had been pulling away lately, spending more time with friends, less time at home. Normal teenage behavior, everyone said. But Marcus's body was preparing for abandonment by creating it first.

"If I push him away now, it won't hurt as much when he leaves for college," Marcus explained in therapy. His unconscious logic was flawed and tragic. By distancing himself from his son, he could control the timing and degree of loss. He wouldn't be blindsided like he was when his parents divorced and his father disappeared.

This is the other side of abandonment schema—the preemptive strike. Some parents cling, others create distance. Both strategies come from the same wound, the same certainty that love equals eventual loss. Parents who can't let children individuate often:

- Had their own independence punished or ignored in childhood
- Experienced sudden, traumatic losses
- Grew up with inconsistent caregivers

- Never learned secure attachment themselves
- Equate separation with permanent loss

The work isn't to force yourself to feel comfortable with separation. It's to recognize when discomfort is schema-based versus situation-based, and to respond to your child's needs rather than your fears.

Recognizing Abandonment Triggers in Daily Parenting

Your schema speaks loudest in ordinary moments. Learning to recognize these triggers is the first step toward responding differently. Common abandonment triggers include:

Morning Separations: School drop-offs, daycare goodbyes, even your child going to another room can activate abandonment fears. You might extend goodbyes, create drama, or feel genuinely panicked.

Preference for Others: When your child runs to the other parent, chooses to sit with someone else, or talks excitedly about a teacher, your schema whispers "you're being replaced."

Normal Anger: Children saying "I hate you," "go away," or "I want daddy/mommy instead" can feel like confirmation of your worst fears rather than normal emotional expression.

Growing Independence: Each milestone—sleeping alone, playing independently, wanting privacy—can trigger grief and panic rather than pride.

End of Day Reunions: If your child doesn't run to greet you or seems happy without having missed you, abandonment schema interprets this as lack of love.

Case Studies in Abandonment Schema

Case Study 1: Sarah's Story Sarah's father died suddenly when she was eight. No goodbye, no preparation, just there one day and gone the next. Forty years later, she found herself creating elaborate goodbye rituals whenever her daughter left for school. "I love you, be careful, text me when you get there, don't forget I'm thinking about you." The mornings were exhausting for both of them.

When her daughter asked to sleep at a friend's house, Sarah's body went into full panic. Racing heart, sweaty palms, catastrophic images. She tried to hide it, but children are emotional detectives. Her daughter started declining invitations, saying "My mom needs me at home." The schema was successfully transmitting itself to the next generation.

In therapy, Sarah learned to recognize her body's alarm signals and use them as information rather than truth. She developed a mantra: "This is sadness about my father, not danger to my daughter." She created new goodbye rituals that were connecting rather than clinging. Most importantly, she started celebrating her daughter's independence as evidence of secure attachment rather than impending loss.

Case Study 2: Marcus's Push-Away Pattern Marcus's parents divorced when he was twelve. His father promised to stay involved but gradually disappeared. Phone calls became less frequent, visits stopped, until there was nothing but silence. Marcus learned that love was something that faded with distance.

With his own son, Marcus unconsciously recreated this pattern. As his son entered adolescence and naturally pulled away, Marcus pulled away further. He worked late, found excuses to miss games, responded to his son's bids for connection with distance. "I'm preparing him for life," he rationalized. "He needs to learn not to depend on anyone."

His wife finally confronted him after their son asked, "Does dad even like me?" Marcus broke down, recognizing his father's pattern in his own behavior. He was abandoning his son before his son could abandon him. With support, Marcus learned to tolerate the discomfort of connection, to stay present even when his schema screamed to run.

Case Study 3: Three Generations of Separation Anxiety In the Martinez family, separation anxiety passed through three generations like a family heirloom nobody wanted. Grandmother Rosa, who fled her country as a child, never let her children out of sight. Mother Elena, raised in this anxiety, developed school phobia and later struggled to let her own daughter, Sofia, develop friendships.

The pattern was consistent: each generation's anxiety created the next generation's struggles. Rosa's hypervigilance taught Elena the world was dangerous. Elena's school phobia taught Sofia that separation caused mom distress. By age seven, Sofia was refusing playdates and clinging to her mother.

The breakthrough came when Elena recognized the pattern during a particularly difficult morning. Sofia was crying about school, Elena was crying about Sofia's distress, and suddenly Elena saw her own mother's face. Three generations of women, all terrified of separation, all creating what they feared most— children who couldn't navigate the world confidently.

Family therapy focused on breaking the pattern at multiple levels. Rosa learned to share stories of strength rather than only fear. Elena worked on her own separation anxiety while supporting Sofia's independence. Sofia learned that she could be safe in the world and her mother would be okay without her.

Practical Exercises

Abandonment Trigger Identification Worksheet

Track your triggers for one week using this format:

1. **Situation**: What happened? (Be specific)
2. **Body Signals**: What did you feel physically?
3. **Thoughts**: What story did your mind tell?
4. **Emotions**: What feelings arose?
5. **Urge**: What did you want to do?
6. **Action**: What did you actually do?
7. **Impact**: How did your child respond?
8. **Schema Link**: How does this connect to your past?

Creating a "Secure Base" Routine for Your Child

Build predictable patterns that communicate "I'm here and you're free to explore":

- **Morning Launch**: "I love you. Have a great day. I'll be here when you get home."
- **After-School Return**: Warm greeting without interrogation. "I'm glad you're home."
- **Bedtime Connection**: 10 minutes of full presence without agenda
- **Weekend Check-ins**: Brief connections between independent activities

Scripts for Healthy Separation (By Age)

Age 3-5: "Mommy/Daddy is going to work. I'll be back after snack time. Ms. Sarah will take good care of you. I love you."

Age 6-8: "Have fun at Emma's house! I'll pick you up tomorrow at 10. If you need me, you can call. Love you!"

Age 9-12: "Enjoy practice. Dad will get you at 5. Text if plans change. Proud of you for trying something new!"

Age 13+: "Have fun tonight. Be home by 10. Make good choices. Love you."

Co-Regulation Techniques for Separation Anxiety

When your child shows separation anxiety, they're borrowing your nervous system. Your calm becomes their calm:

1. **Breathe First**: Three deep breaths before responding
2. **Validate Without Amplifying**: "You're feeling worried. That's okay."
3. **Body Position**: Get on their level, open posture
4. **Confident Voice**: Calm, warm, certain
5. **Brief and Clear**: Don't over-explain or negotiate
6. **Follow Through**: Leave when you say you will

Family Goodbye Rituals That Build Security

Create rituals that connect without clinging:

- **The Secret Handshake**: Quick, special, just for you two
- **The Magic Kiss**: Kiss their hand to "keep" for later
- **The Watching Spot**: Wave from the same window
- **The Comeback Song**: Sing the same short song about returning
- **The Love Note**: Quick note in lunchbox or pocket

Parent-Child Interaction Examples

Morning Drop-Off Scenarios

Age 3 - Preschool Drop-off: Child: "Don't go, Mommy! Stay with me!" Schema Response: "Oh honey, I'll miss you too! Maybe I should stay a little longer. You seem so upset. Are you sure you'll be okay?" Healthy Response: "I know it's hard to say goodbye. I love you and I'll be back after lunch. Give me one big hug, then go show Ms. Amy your new shoes!"

Age 7 - School Drop-off: Child: "My stomach hurts. I think I'm sick." Schema Response: "Oh no! You've been sick a lot lately. Maybe you should stay home. I don't mind. We could spend the day together." Healthy Response: "Sometimes our bellies hurt when we're worried. Let's take three deep breaths together. You've got this! See you at 3:15!"

Age 12 - Activity Drop-off: Child: [Walks away without saying goodbye] Schema Response: "Wait! No hug? Don't you love me anymore? I'll just be sitting in the car if you need me..." Healthy Response: "Have fun!" [Wave and leave, allowing dignity and independence]

Handling "I Hate You" Moments Without Panic

When your child says "I hate you," your abandonment schema hears "I'm leaving you forever." Here's how to respond:

Schema Response: "How can you say that? After everything I do for you? That really hurts my feelings!" Healthy Response: "You're really angry right now. It's okay to be mad. I still love you."

The key is recognizing that children's anger is developmental, not personal. They're practicing emotional expression with the person they feel safest with—you.

Supporting Healthy Friendships Without Jealousy

When your child excitedly talks about a new friend:

Schema Response: "Oh, so Emma is your best friend now? I thought I was your best friend. I guess you don't need me anymore." Healthy Response: "Emma sounds wonderful! I'm so glad you have a good friend. Tell me more about what you like about her."

Healing Strategies

Limited Reparenting Visualization

This technique, drawn from schema therapy[3], helps heal your own abandonment wounds:

1. Close your eyes and picture yourself at the age your abandonment occurred
2. Imagine your adult self entering that scene
3. Give your child self what they needed—presence, reassurance, consistency
4. Stay with the image until your child self feels secure
5. Practice daily, especially when triggered

Challenging Catastrophic Predictions Journal

Keep a record of your fears versus reality:

- **Fear**: "If she goes to the sleepover, something terrible will happen"
- **Reality**: "She went, had fun, came home safely"
- **Learning**: "My fear doesn't predict the future"

Over time, you'll build evidence that separation doesn't equal catastrophe.

Building Your Own Secure Relationships

You can't give what you don't have. Building secure adult relationships helps you model healthy attachment[4]:

- Join a parent support group
- Develop friendships outside your family
- Work on your primary relationship
- Consider therapy for attachment wounds
- Practice asking for help without crisis

Prevention for Children

Age-Appropriate Independence Milestones

- **Age 2-3**: Plays alone for 15-20 minutes
- **Age 4-5**: Stays with familiar caregiver without distress
- **Age 6-7**: Sleepovers with close friends
- **Age 8-9**: Walks to nearby friend's house
- **Age 10-11**: Stays home alone briefly
- **Age 12+**: Increases responsibility gradually

Teaching Emotional Permanence

Help your child understand that love persists across distance:

- Play peek-a-boo (for young children)
- Read books about parents always coming back
- Create photo books of reunions
- Talk about loving someone even when apart
- Point out examples in their experience

Creating Predictable Reunion Rituals

- Same time pickup
- Same greeting style
- Brief connection before questions
- Respect their transition time
- Celebrate their independence

Moving Forward

Sarah now watches her daughter pack for sleepovers with pride instead of panic. She still feels the flutter of fear, but she recognizes it as an echo from the past, not a warning about the present. Marcus plays basketball with his son every weekend, choosing connection over protection from future loss. The

Martinez women are breaking their three-generation pattern one goodbye at a time.

Your abandonment schema will always be part of your story, but it doesn't have to write your child's future. Every time you choose trust over fear, connection over control, faith over panic, you're rewiring not just your brain but your family's emotional legacy. The child who feels free to leave always knows the way home.

Key Takeaways

- **Abandonment schemas create parenting behaviors** that can actually push children away through clinging or preemptive distancing
- **Enmeshment is not love**—healthy attachment allows for both connection and separation
- **Children need secure bases**, not anxious anchors—they must feel free to explore while knowing you're available
- **Common triggers are predictable**—mornings, preferences for others, normal anger, and growing independence
- **Your calm nervous system** regulates your child's anxiety better than any words
- **Healing happens through practice**—each successful separation builds evidence that love survives distance
- **Breaking generational patterns** requires recognizing them in the moment and choosing differently

The next chapter examines what happens when instead of fearing loss, we fear harm—when trust itself feels dangerous and protection becomes prison. But for now, practice one small separation with faith instead of fear. Your child's confident wave goodbye is really saying "I love you enough to leave you, knowing you'll be here when I return."

Chapter 2: When Trust Feels Dangerous - The Mistrust Schema

"Everyone's Out to Get Us"

Michael's jaw clenched as he examined his six-year-old son's knee. Just a scrape from the playground, the teacher had said. But Michael saw more than a simple fall. He saw the push that might have caused it, the supervision that failed to prevent it, the story that didn't quite add up.

"Tell me again what happened," he said, his voice steady but intense. "Where was Mrs. Johnson when you fell? Who else was there? Did anyone push you?"

His son shifted uncomfortably. "I just tripped, Dad. I was running and—"

"You never just trip. Someone did something. Or someone wasn't watching. Tell me the truth, buddy. You can trust me."

The irony of those words—you can trust me—while teaching his son to trust no one else. Michael's childhood had taught him that bruises always had perpetrators, that accidents were cover stories, that the world was full of people waiting to hurt you when your guard dropped[5]. Now, twenty-five years after his own abuse ended, he was scanning his son's world with the same hypervigilance that had once saved him but now threatened to imprison them both.

How Hypervigilance Creates Anxious Children

The mistrust schema operates like a security system that can't be disarmed. Where others see safety, you see potential threat. Where others assume good intentions, you search for hidden agendas. This perpetual state of alert creates a specific kind of family atmosphere—one where danger lurks everywhere and safety exists nowhere.

Children raised in hypervigilant homes develop their own anxiety patterns. They learn to:

- Scan faces for signs of danger
- Question everyone's motives
- Expect betrayal in relationships
- See threat in neutral situations
- Become hypervigilant themselves

The research is clear: children attune to their parents' threat detection systems[6]. If you're constantly on guard, they learn the world requires constant guarding. Your protective instincts, born from real danger in your past, create perceived danger in their present.

What makes this particularly challenging is that hypervigilance feels like good parenting. You're protecting your child, keeping them safe, teaching them to be careful. But there's a profound difference between teaching appropriate caution and transmitting generalized fear.

The Fine Line Between Protection and Paranoia

Anya stood at the park bench, eyes tracking her four-year-old daughter's every movement. She'd already assessed every adult present—the grandmother (seems safe but why is she alone?), the father on his phone (not watching his own kids, definitely not trustworthy), the woman with the dog (dogs can bite).

"Can I go on the big slide?" her daughter called out.

"No, stay where I can see you. And don't talk to anyone."

This had become their routine. Anya within arm's reach, her daughter's world shrinking to match her mother's comfort zone. No playdates (can't trust other parents), no activities without Anya present (coaches could be predators), no family babysitters (family members are often abusers).

Anya's reasoning was flawless if you accepted her premise: danger was everywhere. But in protecting her daughter from hypothetical threats, she was creating actual harm—social isolation, excessive dependency, and the early seeds of her own mistrust schema.

Here's how to recognize when protection crosses into paranoia:

Healthy Protection:

- Based on realistic assessment of actual risk
- Allows for age-appropriate independence
- Teaches skills for safety
- Flexible based on context
- Builds confidence alongside caution

Paranoid Protection:

- Based on worst-case scenario thinking
- Restricts normal development
- Teaches fear as primary response
- Rigid regardless of circumstances
- Creates dependency and anxiety

Teaching Discernment vs. Universal Distrust

The goal isn't to raise naive children who trust everyone. The goal is to raise children who can accurately assess situations and respond appropriately. This requires teaching discernment—the ability to distinguish between actual threat and general existence.

Consider these two approaches to the same situation:

Universal Distrust Approach: "Don't trust your teacher. Teachers lie. If she says something that doesn't feel right, you tell me immediately. People in authority abuse their power. Always be careful what you say to her."

Discernment Approach: "Your teacher is there to help you learn. Most teachers care about kids. If something ever feels uncomfortable or confusing, you can always talk to me about it. Let's practice knowing when to ask for help."

One approach creates a child who sees enemies everywhere. The other creates a child who can navigate relationships while maintaining appropriate boundaries.

Breaking the Victim-Perpetrator Cycle

When you've been hurt by others, the world divides into two categories: victims and perpetrators. You're determined your child won't be a victim, but in that determination, you might unconsciously create the very dynamic you're trying to avoid.

The victim-perpetrator cycle in families looks like:

- Seeing all conflicts through the lens of power and abuse
- Teaching children they're either hurting or being hurt
- Missing the middle ground of mutual relationships
- Creating self-fulfilling prophecies of betrayal
- Passing on a worldview of inevitable harm

Breaking this cycle requires adding a third category: people navigating relationships imperfectly but without malicious intent. Most playground conflicts aren't bullying. Most teacher corrections aren't abuse. Most friendship struggles aren't betrayal. They're humans learning to be together.

27

Case Studies in Mistrust Schema

Case Study 1: Michael's Interrogation Pattern Michael survived severe physical abuse from ages 5 to 12. His stepfather was charming in public, violent in private. Teachers missed the signs. Neighbors looked away. Michael learned that bruises meant secrets and adults couldn't be trusted to protect children.

Now, every mark on his son triggered a full investigation. "Who did this? What really happened? Are you protecting someone?" His son began hiding normal childhood injuries—scrapes from bike rides, bruises from soccer. He learned that injuries upset Dad, that Dad saw danger everywhere, that maybe the world really was as dangerous as Dad believed.

The turning point came when Michael's son fell at school and begged the nurse not to call his father. "He'll think someone hurt me," the boy cried. The nurse, trained in trauma-informed care, recognized the pattern and gently suggested family counseling.

In therapy, Michael learned to separate his past from his son's present. He developed a protocol: First, comfort. Second, basic facts. Third, pause before pursuing further. Most importantly, he began sharing age-appropriate truths: "When I was little, someone hurt me, so sometimes I worry too much about you getting hurt. But your world is different from mine."

Case Study 2: Anya's Isolation Strategy Anya's mother had been sexually abused by a babysitter. The story was family legend—trusted neighbor, devastating betrayal, lifelong trauma. Anya absorbed the lesson: caregivers were dangerous, isolation was safety.

By the time her daughter was four, their world had shrunk to just the two of them. No babysitters, no preschool, no playdates. Anya worked from home to maintain constant supervision. She saw this as devotion. Others saw a child with no social skills and a mother consumed by fear.

The isolation broke when Anya had a medical emergency and no one to watch her daughter. Her neighbor—whom she'd avoided for years—stepped in. Her daughter thrived in those few hours, playing with the neighbor's children, laughing in ways Anya hadn't heard before.

Watching her daughter's joy with other children awakened something in Anya. She realized her protection had become a prison. Therapy helped her develop a gradual exposure plan: supervised playdates, then short separations, eventually preschool with extensive vetting. Each successful experience built evidence that catastrophe wasn't inevitable.

Case Study 3: Twin Outcomes The Chen twins, David and Daniel, grew up with a father whose mistrust schema dominated family life. Every friend was scrutinized, every teacher suspected, every activity evaluated for potential harm. The twins, identical in appearance, developed opposite responses.

David internalized the mistrust. By high school, he had no close friends, suspected classmates of stealing when items were misplaced, and interpreted neutral interactions as hostile. He was safe but profoundly lonely.

Daniel rebelled against it. He trusted everyone, almost defiantly. He overshared personal information, ignored red flags in relationships, and seemed determined to prove his father wrong by being maximally vulnerable.

Both responses were schema-driven, just in different directions. David replicated the schema perfectly. Daniel developed what's called a "compensation" pattern—going to the opposite extreme to avoid the pain of mistrust.

Family therapy revealed how both boys were trapped by their father's schema. David needed to learn calculated trust. Daniel needed to develop appropriate caution. Their father needed to see how his protection had created two different but equally problematic patterns.

Practical Exercises

Trust Assessment Scale for Different Relationships

Create a realistic trust scale from 1-10 for various relationships:

1-3: **Low Trust** (Strangers, new acquaintances)

- Share basic information only
- Maintain boundaries
- Observe behavior over time

4-6: **Moderate Trust** (Colleagues, neighbors, casual friends)

- Share some personal information
- Accept help with verification
- Build slowly based on consistency

7-9: **High Trust** (Close friends, family, proven relationships)

- Share vulnerabilities appropriately
- Accept help freely
- Allow influence on decisions

10: **Complete Trust** (Should be very rare)

- Reserved for most intimate relationships
- Built over years of consistency
- Still maintains healthy boundaries

Creating a "Safety Network" Map with Children

Draw concentric circles with your child:

- **Center Circle**: Immediate family
- **Second Circle**: Extended family and close friends
- **Third Circle**: Teachers, coaches, familiar adults
- **Fourth Circle**: Acquaintances
- **Outer Circle**: Strangers

Discuss appropriate interactions for each circle. This visual helps children understand that trust exists on a spectrum, not as an all-or-nothing proposition.

Age-Appropriate Stranger Danger Talks

Ages 3-5: "Most people are kind and helpful. If you're ever lost or scared, look for a mommy with children or someone working in a store. Don't go anywhere with someone you don't know unless Mommy or Daddy said it's okay."

Ages 6-8: "Your body belongs to you. Safe grown-ups don't ask children to keep secrets from parents. If anyone makes you feel uncomfortable, even someone we know, you can always tell me. I'll always believe you."

Ages 9-12: "As you get more independent, you'll meet more people. Trust your instincts. If something feels off, it probably is. You can always call me, no questions asked, if you need help."

Repairing After Schema-Driven Overreactions

When you've responded from mistrust rather than reality:

1. **Acknowledge**: "I reacted too strongly. That was about my worries, not about what actually happened."
2. **Apologize**: "I'm sorry I interrogated you. You didn't deserve that."

3. **Explain** (age-appropriately): "Sometimes I worry too much because of things that happened when I was young."
4. **Reassure**: "I'm working on this. You're safe and I trust you."
5. **Reconnect**: Do something enjoyable together to restore connection

Building Trust Incrementally Worksheet

Track trust-building experiences:

- **Person/Situation**: Who or what are you practicing trusting?
- **Prediction**: What does your schema predict will happen?
- **Actual Outcome**: What actually happened?
- **Learning**: What does this teach about your schema versus reality?
- **Next Step**: How can you build on this?

Parent-Child Interaction Examples

Handling Reports of Peer Conflict Without Panic

Child: "James pushed me at recess today."

Mistrust Response: "He pushed you? That's assault! Who saw it? What did the teacher do? This is exactly what I was afraid of. We're calling the principal right now. Maybe we should switch schools."

Balanced Response: "That must have been upsetting. Tell me what happened. How did you handle it? Do you need help figuring out what to do next?"

Teaching Body Safety Without Creating Fear

Mistrust Approach: "Never let anyone touch you. People who want to touch children are everywhere. If anyone even looks at you wrong, you run and scream. Trust no one."

Balanced Approach: "Your body belongs to you. Safe touches are ones that make you feel happy and comfortable, like hugs from people you love. If anyone touches you in a way that feels uncomfortable or confusing, you can always tell me."

Supporting Teacher Relationships Despite Your Mistrust

When meeting your child's new teacher:

Mistrust Approach: Interrogate about credentials, demand constant updates, express suspicion about methods, undermine authority at home.

Balanced Approach: Share relevant information about your child, establish communication preferences, support the teacher-child relationship while staying involved, address concerns directly and respectfully.

Healing Strategies

EMDR or Trauma Therapy Resources

If your mistrust stems from trauma, specialized therapy can help[7]:

- EMDR helps reprocess traumatic memories
- Trauma-focused CBT addresses thought patterns
- Somatic therapies work with body-based responses
- Group therapy provides corrective experiences

The goal isn't to forget what happened but to stop living as if it's still happening.

Gradual Exposure to Trusting Others

Start small:

1. Let a trusted friend help with something minor
2. Accept a favor without investigating motives
3. Share a small vulnerability
4. Allow your child a supervised playdate
5. Build on each success

Creating Corrective Experiences

Actively seek experiences that contradict your schema:

- Notice when people are trustworthy
- Document positive interactions
- Celebrate when trust is rewarded
- Share these experiences with your child

Prevention for Children

Teaching Healthy Caution vs. Paranoia

Healthy caution says:

- Pay attention to your feelings
- Most people are safe, some aren't
- You can ask for help when needed
- Trust builds over time
- You have good instincts

Paranoia says:

- Everyone is suspicious
- Assume bad intentions
- You're always in danger
- Never let your guard down

- The world is against you

Modeling Appropriate Trust

Children learn trust by watching you:

- Accept help gracefully
- Assume positive intent initially
- Address conflicts directly
- Maintain friendships
- Show faith in systems and people

Building Social Connections Safely

- Start with structured activities
- Build relationships gradually
- Teach social skills explicitly
- Process experiences together
- Celebrate successful connections

Looking Ahead

Michael now watches his son play without interrogating every interaction. He still notices the scrapes and bruises, but he's learned to pause before pursuing conspiracy theories. Anya's daughter attends preschool three days a week—a victory that once seemed impossible. The Chen twins are finding their balance, learning that trust isn't all or nothing but a skill to be developed.

Your mistrust schema protected you once. It kept you vigilant when vigilance was necessary, suspicious when suspicion was warranted. But your child lives in a different world than the one that hurt you. They need your wisdom about safety without your certainty about danger. Every time you choose curiosity over suspicion, connection over isolation, measured trust over absolute mistrust, you're giving your child the freedom to form their own relationships with appropriate caution rather than inherited fear.

Key Takeaways

- **Hypervigilance is contagious**—children absorb parental anxiety and threat detection patterns
- **Protection becomes harmful** when it prevents normal social development and creates isolation
- **Discernment differs from distrust**—teach children to assess situations rather than assume danger
- **The victim-perpetrator cycle** limits relationship possibilities to hurting or being hurt
- **Mistrust creates self-fulfilling prophecies**—expecting betrayal often leads to behaviors that invite it
- **Gradual exposure builds evidence** that catastrophic betrayal isn't inevitable
- **Children need to see you trust** appropriately to learn that relationships can be safe

The path from mistrust to measured trust isn't straight. You'll have setbacks, moments of panic, times when old patterns feel safer than new possibilities. But each small act of faith—each playdate permitted, each teacher trusted, each friendship supported—rewires both your nervous system and your child's developing worldview. In the next chapter, we'll explore what happens when the absence isn't about safety or presence, but about emotional connection itself.

Chapter 3: When Hearts Stay Hidden - The Emotional Deprivation Schema

"I Love You, I Just Can't Show It"

Jennifer sat on the edge of her daughter's bed, watching tears stream down the seven-year-old's face. The sobs came in waves—something about a best friend who didn't want to play anymore, words that hurt, the crushing weight of childhood social pain. Jennifer's mind raced through solutions: call the other parent, switch schools, arrange new playdates. Anything but this.

"Maybe you could..." she began, then stopped. Her daughter wasn't looking for solutions. She was looking for something Jennifer didn't know how to give. The child reached out her arms, and Jennifer's body stiffened involuntarily. She patted her daughter's shoulder—two quick taps, efficient and brief—then stood abruptly.

"You'll feel better tomorrow," Jennifer said, switching off the light. "Get some sleep."

In the hallway, she leaned against the wall, heart pounding. She'd provided everything—the best schools, tutors, activities, organic meals. She'd never missed a recital or parent conference. She loved her daughter fiercely. So why did holding her crying child feel like drowning?

Why Some Parents Can't Attune Emotionally

Emotional attunement is the ability to sense, understand, and respond to another person's emotional state. For parents with emotional deprivation schemas, this feels like speaking a foreign language they never learned. The schema typically develops when:

- Caregivers met physical needs but ignored emotional ones
- Emotions were seen as weakness or inconvenience
- Love was expressed through provision, not connection
- Children learned to suppress needs to avoid disappointment
- Emotional expression was punished or dismissed

The result is adults who genuinely love their children but literally don't know how to show it in ways children can feel. They become parents who say "I love you" while maintaining physical distance, who provide abundantly while connecting rarely, who would die for their children but can't comfort them when they cry.

Research on emotional neglect shows it can be as damaging as active abuse[8]. Children need emotional attunement like plants need water. Without it, they wilt in ways that might not show immediately but shape their entire emotional architecture.

The Difference Between Providing and Nurturing

Jennifer's confusion is common among parents with this schema. She's doing everything "right"—so why does her daughter seem emotionally hungry? The answer lies in understanding the difference between providing and nurturing.

Providing looks like:

- Meeting physical needs (food, shelter, clothing)
- Ensuring educational opportunities
- Arranging activities and experiences
- Solving practical problems
- Giving things instead of presence

Nurturing looks like:

- Making eye contact during emotional moments
- Using touch to comfort and connect
- Reflecting feelings back ("You seem sad")
- Sharing your own emotions appropriately
- Being present without fixing

Providing says "I'll take care of you." Nurturing says "I see you, I feel with you, we're in this together." Children need both, but emotional deprivation schema makes nurturing feel impossible, unnecessary, or dangerous.

Consider how differently these two responses land for a child:

Providing Response: "You're upset about your friend. Let me call her mom and sort this out. Maybe we should find you some new friends. I'll sign you up for that art class you wanted."

Nurturing Response: "Oh sweetheart, that really hurt your feelings. Come here. Tell me all about it. Sometimes friends can be mean without meaning to. I'm so sorry this happened."

One tries to fix, the other connects. One avoids the emotion, the other enters it. One leaves the child alone with their feelings, the other joins them there.

How Children Interpret Emotional Absence

Children are meaning-making machines. When emotional connection is absent, they don't think "My parent has an emotional deprivation schema." They create stories to explain the absence, and these stories become their schemas[9].

Common interpretations include:

- "My feelings don't matter"
- "I'm too much/too needy"
- "Love means things, not connection"

- "Emotions are dangerous/shameful"
- "I must handle everything alone"

David discovered this when his eight-year-old son started having nightmares. "I'm fine," the boy insisted, tears still wet on his cheeks. "I don't need anything." The words were eerily familiar—David had said them throughout his own childhood. His son had learned that emotional needs wouldn't be met, so he'd stopped expressing them.

Children of emotionally deprived parents often become:

- Hyper-independent (can't rely on others)
- Emotionally shut down (why feel if no one responds?)
- Anxiously attached (desperate for connection)
- Caregivers to their parents (role reversal)
- Perfectionists (maybe achievement earns connection)

Breaking the "Strong and Silent" Generational Pattern

Many families pass emotional deprivation through generations like a twisted heirloom. "We're not huggers," they say. "We don't do emotions." "We're strong." But strength without softness isn't strength—it's armor that keeps love out along with pain.

The pattern often looks like:

- Grandparents who showed love through hard work
- Parents who show love through provision
- Children who don't feel loved at all
- Each generation getting technically "better" but emotionally emptier

Breaking this pattern requires conscious choice and daily practice. It means:

1. Acknowledging the pattern exists
2. Grieving what you didn't receive
3. Learning emotional skills as an adult
4. Practicing with safe people first
5. Gradually bringing these skills to parenting

Case Studies in Emotional Deprivation Schema

Case Study 1: Jennifer's Executive Freeze Jennifer ran a Fortune 500 division. She could face hostile boardrooms, make million-dollar decisions, manage hundreds of employees. But her daughter's tears paralyzed her.

Growing up, Jennifer's mother had been efficient, organized, and utterly unavailable emotionally. "Stop crying or I'll give you something to cry about" was the family motto. Love meant clean clothes, good grades, and no complaints. Jennifer learned to need nothing, feel nothing, expect nothing emotionally.

Now, her daughter's emotional needs triggered panic. The child's tears felt like criticism—proof Jennifer was failing. Her body literally couldn't stay present for emotions because it had never learned how. She'd dissociate, make lists in her head, or suddenly need to check email.

The breakthrough came when her daughter wrote a school essay titled "My Mom." It described all the things Jennifer provided, ending with "I know she loves me because she does so much for me. I just wish she would hug me sometimes."

Jennifer sobbed—alone, of course. Then she got help.

Case Study 2: David's Emotional Illiteracy David's family took pride in being "logical." His engineer father and scientist mother discussed ideas, not feelings. When David fell and cried as a child, they'd explain why crying didn't help. When he was scared, they'd list statistics about actual versus perceived danger.

Now David had an intensely emotional son. The boy felt everything deeply—joy that bubbled over, sadness that consumed him, anger that exploded. David watched helplessly, like someone at an opera sung in a language he didn't understand.

"Use your words," he'd tell his crying son, not realizing the child was using the only words he had—tears. David would offer solutions, distractions, logic, anything but emotional presence. His son began having behavioral problems, which David approached like engineering problems to solve.

The turning point came during a parent-teacher conference. "Your son told me he feels like a robot," the teacher said gently. "He said that's what his dad wants—for him to not feel things." David realized he was programming his son to be as emotionally shut down as he was.

Case Study 3: The Martinez Family Learning Together The Martinez family represented three generations of emotional deprivation. Grandmother Elena, raised in poverty, equated love with sacrifice. Mother Sofia, raised by Elena, equated love with achievement. Eight-year-old Lucia was anxious, perfectionistic, and desperately lonely despite being surrounded by family who loved her.

Family therapy revealed a pattern: each generation loved deeply but couldn't express it directly. Elena cooked elaborate meals but couldn't say "I love you." Sofia drove Lucia to endless activities but couldn't sit still for bedtime cuddles. Lucia excelled at everything but felt empty inside.

Their therapist introduced "emotion practice" as a family. They started with naming feelings using a chart. Then graduated to sharing one feeling at dinner. Eventually, they learned to comfort each other physically—awkward hugs that slowly became natural.

The breakthrough moment came when Lucia had a bad day at school. Instead of offering solutions or distractions, Sofia sat with her, held her, and said, "Tell me everything. I'm here." Elena watched from the doorway, then joined them, three generations learning emotional connection together.

Practical Exercises

Emotion Identification Practice for Parents

Start with yourself before you can help your child:

1. **Body Scan**: Three times daily, pause and notice:
   - Where do you feel tension?
   - What's your breathing like?
   - What physical sensations are present?
2. **Feeling Wheel**: Use an emotion wheel chart to identify specific feelings beyond "fine" or "okay"
3. **Emotion Journal**: Each night, write:
   - One emotion you felt today
   - Where you felt it in your body
   - What triggered it
   - How you expressed (or didn't express) it

Daily Emotional Check-In Templates

Morning Check-In: "Good morning! How are you feeling today? Is your heart happy, sad, worried, or something else?"

After School Check-In: "Tell me about your day. What was the best part? Was there a hard part? How did that make you feel?"

Bedtime Check-In: "Before we read stories, let's share our feelings from today. I felt _____ when _____. What about you?"

Creating "Feeling-Safe" Spaces at Home

Designate spaces where emotions are welcome:

- **The Comfort Corner**: Soft pillows, stuffed animals, feeling books
- **The Mad Pad**: Safe space for anger with foam bats, paper to rip
- **The Worry Window**: Place to draw or write worries
- **The Joy Jar**: Collection of happy memories to share

Emotional Vocabulary Building (By Age)

Ages 2-4: Happy, sad, mad, scared, excited *Ages 5-7:* Add frustrated, disappointed, proud, jealous, worried *Ages 8-10:* Add embarrassed, guilty, confident, anxious, grateful *Ages 11+:* Add complex emotions like ambivalent, melancholy, content

Use these in natural conversation: "You look frustrated. Is that right?"

Rupture and Repair Practice Scenarios

When you miss emotional cues, repair quickly:

1. **Acknowledge**: "I noticed you were sad earlier and I didn't stop to listen."
2. **Apologize**: "I'm sorry. Your feelings matter to me."
3. **Invite**: "Would you like to tell me about it now?"
4. **Connect**: Use eye contact, appropriate touch, full presence
5. **Appreciate**: "Thank you for sharing with me."

Parent-Child Interaction Examples

Bedtime Emotional Connection Rituals

Create consistent routines that invite emotional sharing:

The Rose and Thorn: "Tell me your rose (best part) and thorn (hard part) from today."

The Feeling Story: "Once upon a time, there was a little girl who felt... [let child fill in]"

The Heart Share: "Let's put our hands on our hearts and share what's inside."

Responding to "Mom, I'm Sad" at Different Ages

Age 3: Child: "Mommy, I sad." Emotionally Deprived Response: "You're okay. Want a snack?" Connected Response: "Oh, you're sad. Come here, sweetie. Tell Mommy why."

Age 7: Child: "I'm sad and I don't know why." Emotionally Deprived Response: "Well, you have nothing to be sad about. Look at all your toys." Connected Response: "Sometimes we feel sad without knowing why. That's okay. Want to sit with me?"

Age 12: Child: "Just leave me alone. I'm sad, okay?" Emotionally Deprived Response: "Fine. Let me know when you're ready to be pleasant." Connected Response: "I hear you. I'm here when you're ready. Would a hug help or would space feel better?"

Validating Feelings During Tantrums

The emotional deprivation response to tantrums is often to shut them down quickly. The connected response acknowledges the feeling while maintaining boundaries:

Emotionally Deprived Response: "Stop crying right now! Go to your room until you can control yourself!"

Connected Response: "You're so angry that you can't have the toy. I get it. It's hard when we can't have what we want. I'll stay here with you while you feel your big feelings."

Healing Strategies

Emotion-Focused Therapy Techniques

EFT helps you access and express emotions safely[10]:

- **Two-Chair Work**: Dialogue between emotional and logical parts
- **Empty Chair**: Express feelings to absent caregivers
- **Focusing**: Learn to sense emotions in your body
- **Emotional Processing**: Slow down to feel rather than think

Mindfulness for Emotional Awareness

Simple practices to build emotional presence:

1. **STOP Practice**:
   - Stop what you're doing
   - Take a breath
   - Observe your inner state
   - Proceed with awareness
2. **Loving-Kindness Meditation**: Start with yourself, then extend to your child
3. **Body-Based Awareness**: Notice where emotions live in your body

Learning Your Emotional Triggers

Map what shuts you down emotionally:

- Crying children (reminds you of being told not to cry)
- Anger (feels dangerous based on past)

- Neediness (triggers your own unmet needs)
- Joy (feels unsafe to feel too good)

Once mapped, you can prepare strategies for each trigger.

Prevention for Children

Teaching Emotional Literacy Early

- Read books about feelings daily
- Name emotions as they happen
- Model emotional expression
- Celebrate emotional awareness
- Never shame emotional expression

Modeling Emotional Expression

Children learn by watching. Let them see you:

- Cry during sad movies
- Express frustration appropriately
- Share when you're worried
- Celebrate joyfully
- Apologize when you mess up

Creating Family Sharing Rituals

- Weekly family feelings meeting
- Emotion charades game
- Feeling faces photo album
- Gratitude practice at meals
- Bedtime appreciation circle

The Path Forward

Jennifer now holds her daughter when she cries. It still feels uncomfortable, but she's learned that comfort isn't the goal—

connection is. David and his son have "feeling time" each night, learning emotional vocabulary together. The Martinez family continues their journey, three generations healing together.

Your emotional deprivation schema isn't your fault. You can't give what you never received. But you can learn. Every time you stay present for an emotion—yours or your child's—you're rewriting generational code. Every awkward hug, every stumbling attempt to reflect feelings, every moment you choose connection over efficiency is revolutionary.

Your children don't need perfect emotional attunement. They need "good enough" emotional presence—a parent who's learning, trying, staying in the room even when it's hard. That parent is you, one feeling at a time.

Key Takeaways

- **Emotional deprivation schema** creates parents who love deeply but can't express it in ways children can feel
- **Providing differs from nurturing**—children need emotional presence, not just physical provision
- **Children interpret emotional absence** as their own failing, creating future schemas
- **Breaking generational patterns** requires learning emotional skills as adults
- **Small moments of connection** matter more than grand gestures
- **Repair is always possible**—it's never too late to start connecting emotionally
- **Progress over perfection**—awkward attempts at emotion are better than smooth avoidance

Chapter 4: When Shame Runs Deep - The Defectiveness Schema

"What's Wrong With You?" vs. "What Happened to You?"

Maria heard the words leave her mouth and immediately wanted to pull them back. But they hung in the air between her and her ten-year-old son like a toxic cloud. "What is wrong with you? Why can't you just be normal like other kids?"

Her son's face crumbled, and in that destruction, Maria saw her own childhood reflection. She was eight again, standing in her family's kitchen while her mother listed all the ways she was defective, disappointing, not enough. The cycle was spinning forward, one generation to the next, shame passing through families like a cursed inheritance.

"I'm sorry," Maria whispered, but the damage was done. Her son had already absorbed the message that schemas ensure gets transmitted: there's something fundamentally wrong with you, and everyone can see it.

How Parental Shame Becomes Child Shame

Shame is different from guilt. Guilt says "I did something bad." Shame says "I am bad." When parents carry defectiveness schemas, they transmit shame like a virus, infecting their children with the same sense of being fundamentally flawed[11].

The transmission happens through:

- **Direct criticism**: "What's wrong with you?" "Why can't you be more like...?"
- **Comparison**: Constantly measuring against others
- **Perfectionism**: Nothing is ever good enough

- **Emotional rejection**: Withdrawing love when child disappoints
- **Public humiliation**: Shaming in front of others
- **Global statements**: "You always..." "You never..."

Children don't have the cognitive ability to think, "My parent has unresolved shame issues." They believe what they're told about themselves. If the most important person in their world says they're defective, it must be true.

Research on shame shows it actually changes brain development, affecting areas responsible for self-concept and emotional regulation[12]. Children who internalize shame develop their own defectiveness schemas, continuing the cycle.

The Critical Inner Voice That Criticizes Your Child

James watched his daughter struggle with her math homework. She erased her answer for the third time, and he felt the familiar surge of frustration. But underneath that frustration was something deeper—shame. Her struggle triggered his own memories of being "stupid at math," of his father's disgusted sighs, of feeling fundamentally inadequate.

"This is simple multiplication," he snapped. "What aren't you getting?"

His critical voice wasn't really about his daughter's math skills. It was his own inner critic, projected outward. Parents with defectiveness schemas often have brutal inner critics that attack not just themselves but their children. The critic says:

- "She's lazy" (because I was called lazy)
- "He's not trying" (because I was never good enough)
- "They're embarrassing me" (because I was shameful)
- "Something's wrong with them" (because something's wrong with me)

The inner critic speaks loudest when children's behavior triggers parents' own shame. A child's mistake becomes evidence of parental failure. A child's struggle confirms the parent's deepest fear—that their defectiveness has been passed on.

Perfectionism as a Shame Defense

Many parents with defectiveness schemas develop perfectionism as armor against shame[13]. If everything is perfect, no one can see the flaws. But perfectionism in parenting creates its own damage:

The Perfect Parent Trap:

- Never admitting mistakes
- Presenting flawless family image
- Hiding all struggles
- Demanding perfection from children
- Treating mistakes as catastrophes

The Perfect Child Pressure:

- Academic perfection expected
- Behavioral perfection demanded
- Appearance standards enforced
- Achievement as worth measure
- Mistakes hidden or punished

Maria's family looked perfect from outside—honor roll students, coordinated outfits, Facebook-worthy moments. But inside, everyone was drowning in shame. The perfection was exhausting to maintain and impossible to achieve, creating more shame when anyone inevitably fell short.

Creating a Shame-Resilient Family Culture

Brené Brown defines shame resilience as the ability to recognize shame, move through it constructively, and grow from the experience[14]. Creating this culture requires:

1. **Normalizing imperfection**: "Everyone makes mistakes"
2. **Separating behavior from identity**: "You made a poor choice" vs. "You're bad"
3. **Modeling self-compassion**: Treating yourself kindly when you fail
4. **Celebrating effort over outcome**: "I'm proud of how hard you tried"
5. **Creating repair culture**: Mistakes are opportunities to reconnect

A shame-resilient family says:

- "Mistakes are how we learn"
- "You are loved no matter what"
- "Let's figure this out together"
- "Your worth isn't measured by achievement"
- "We all struggle sometimes"

Case Studies in Defectiveness Schema

Case Study 1: Maria's Critical Voice Heritage Maria's mother had been the family shame-keeper. Nothing was ever good enough—Maria's grades (why not straight A's?), her appearance (you'd be pretty if...), her friends (not the right kind). Love felt conditional on impossible standards.

Now Maria heard her mother's voice coming from her own mouth. When her son struggled socially, she felt exposed, as if his awkwardness revealed her defectiveness. She'd critique his interactions: "Why did you say that? Don't you know how weird that sounds?"

The breakthrough came at a school event. Maria watched her son standing alone, shoulders hunched in the same shame posture she recognized from her own childhood photos. She saw the generational pattern physically manifested—grandmother, mother, son, all carrying the same bodily shame.

That night, Maria apologized deeply. "I've been putting my fears on you. You're not weird. You're wonderful. I'm sorry I made you feel otherwise." They began working together to break the pattern.

Case Study 2: James's Triggered Shame James was a successful surgeon who'd never felt successful enough. His daughter's learning disability triggered every message he'd received about being "slow" before his dyslexia was diagnosed. Watching her struggle with reading transported him back to classroom humiliation.

Instead of empathy, he responded with anger—the same anger his father had shown. "You're not trying hard enough. You're being lazy. What's wrong with you?" Each criticism deepened his daughter's shame while confirming his own sense of defectiveness.

His wife finally intervened after finding their daughter's journal. She'd written: "Dad thinks I'm stupid. Maybe I am. I wish I was dead so I wouldn't disappoint him anymore."

James broke down completely. In therapy, he connected his treatment of his daughter to his own childhood wounds. He began sharing his own struggles with her: "I have trouble reading too. It doesn't mean we're broken. Our brains just work differently."

Case Study 3: Breaking Three Generations of Shame The Thompson family represented three generations of shame transmission. Grandfather Robert, raised during the Depression, believed showing weakness was shameful. His son Michael learned emotions were defective. Michael's daughter Emma, age 12, was developing an eating disorder, trying to perfect her body to earn love.

Family therapy revealed how shame had morphed through generations:

- Robert shamed emotional expression
- Michael shamed imperfection
- Emma shamed her own existence

The therapist introduced "shame interruption" practices. When someone started shaming themselves or others, anyone could call "pause" and redirect to compassion. They practiced daily:

Robert learned to say "I felt scared" instead of "Real men don't fear" Michael learned to say "This is hard for me" instead of demanding perfection Emma learned she was lovable as-is, not as-perfect

The work was slow, but shame's grip loosened with each honest conversation.

Practical Exercises

Identifying Your "Shame Triggers" as a Parent

Track for one week what child behaviors trigger your shame:

1. **Behavior**: What did your child do?
2. **Your Response**: What did you say/do?
3. **Body Sensation**: Where did you feel it?
4. **Memory Echo**: What childhood moment did it recall?
5. **Shame Message**: What story about defectiveness arose?

Common triggers include:

- Public misbehavior (they're exposing my bad parenting)
- Academic struggles (they inherited my defects)
- Social difficulties (they're weird like I was)
- Emotional expression (they're too much)
- Independence (they don't need me)

Rewriting Critical Scripts into Teaching Moments

Transform shame-based responses into growth-focused ones:

Shame Script: "What's wrong with you? Can't you do anything right?" *Teaching Script*: "That didn't work out. What could we try differently?"

Shame Script: "You're so lazy. You'll never amount to anything." *Teaching Script*: "I notice you're struggling to get started. What would help?"

Shame Script: "Why can't you be more like your sister?" *Teaching Script*: "Everyone has different strengths. What are yours?"

Mistake Repair Protocols for the Family

Create a family practice for when shame takes over:

1. **Pause**: Stop the shame spiral
2. **Breathe**: Everyone takes three breaths
3. **Own**: Parent acknowledges what happened
4. **Repair**: Apologize specifically
5. **Reconnect**: Physical touch if welcomed
6. **Learn**: What will we do differently?

Building a "Good Enough" Parenting Practice

Replace perfectionism with "good enough"[15]:

- Celebrate meeting basic needs
- Accept messy houses mean playing happened
- Value connection over appearance
- Share your struggles with trusted friends
- Model self-forgiveness daily

Good enough says:

- "I showed up"
- "I tried my best today"
- "Tomorrow is a new chance"
- "Love matters more than perfection"
- "We're all learning together"

Celebration Practices for Effort Over Outcome

- **Effort Board**: Display attempts, not just achievements
- **Failure Parties**: Celebrate spectacular failures as brave attempts
- **Process Praise**: "I saw how hard you concentrated"
- **Growth Tracking**: Compare to previous self, not others
- **Courage Cards**: Write notes celebrating brave attempts

Parent-Child Interaction Examples

Responding to Report Cards Without Shame

Child brings home B's and C's

Shame Response: "These grades are unacceptable. What will people think? You're smarter than this. I'm so disappointed in you."

Resilient Response: "Thanks for showing me your report card. I see some subjects are going well and others are harder. How do you feel about it? What support would help?"

Handling Public Misbehavior with Dignity

Child has meltdown in store

Shame Response: "Stop it right now! You're embarrassing me! What's wrong with you? Everyone's watching!"

Resilient Response: [Calmly] "You're having a hard time. Let's go to the car where it's quieter." [Later] "That was tough for both of us. What was happening for you?"

Teaching Accountability Without Shame

Child lies about homework

Shame Response: "You're a liar! I can't trust anything you say! What kind of person lies to their mother?"

Resilient Response: "I know you didn't do your homework. Help me understand what made it hard to tell me the truth. Let's figure out a plan that works better."

Healing Strategies

Self-Compassion Practices

Kristin Neff's self-compassion framework includes[16]:

1. **Mindfulness**: Notice shame without drowning in it
2. **Common Humanity**: Everyone struggles and fails
3. **Self-Kindness**: Treat yourself as you would a good friend

Daily practice:

- Morning affirmation: "I am enough as I am"
- Mistake mantra: "I'm human and I'm learning"

- Evening reflection: "What can I appreciate about myself today?"

Challenging the Inner Critic

When the critic attacks you or your child:

1. **Name it**: "That's my shame voice talking"
2. **Question it**: "Is this absolutely true?"
3. **Evidence check**: "What proves otherwise?"
4. **Reframe**: "What would compassion say?"
5. **Choose**: "Which voice will I act from?"

Creating New Family Narratives

Replace shame stories with strength stories:

Old Narrative: "We're just not math people" *New Narrative*: "We work hard at challenging things"

Old Narrative: "Our family is messy and chaotic" *New Narrative*: "Our family is creative and full of life"

Old Narrative: "We always screw things up" *New Narrative*: "We learn from mistakes and keep trying"

Prevention for Children

Separating Behavior from Identity

Always distinguish between what children do and who they are:

- "You hit your sister" NOT "You're violent"
- "You didn't tell the truth" NOT "You're a liar"
- "You made a poor choice" NOT "You're bad"
- "That behavior isn't okay" NOT "You're not okay"

Teaching Healthy Guilt vs. Toxic Shame

Help children understand the difference:

Healthy Guilt: "I did something that hurt someone. I can make amends and do better next time."

Toxic Shame: "I am bad and wrong. Nothing I do will change that."

Model healthy guilt: "I spoke harshly to you. I feel bad about that because it hurt you. I'm sorry. Next time I'll take a breath first."

Modeling Self-Compassion

Let children see you treat yourself kindly:

- "I made a mistake. That's okay, I'm learning"
- "I'm struggling today and that's human"
- "I don't have to be perfect to be lovable"
- "I'm proud of myself for trying"

The Courage to Transform

Maria now catches her mother's voice before it escapes her mouth. She's teaching her son that mistakes are data, not disasters. James shares his reading struggles with his daughter, showing her that different doesn't mean defective. The Thompson family practices shame interruption daily, three generations learning together that love doesn't require perfection.

Your defectiveness schema tells lies about you and your children. Every time you choose compassion over criticism, acceptance over perfectionism, "what happened to you?" over "what's wrong with you?"—you're rewriting your family's story.

Shame thrives in silence and secrecy. It cannot survive being spoken, witnessed, and met with love.

Your children need to see you struggling and surviving, failing and recovering, being imperfect and still worthy of love. They need to know that their worth isn't measured in achievements or compliance but in their inherent humanity. This is how shame ends—one compassionate response at a time.

Key Takeaways

- **Shame is transmitted intergenerationally** through criticism, comparison, and conditional love
- **The inner critic attacks our children** when their behavior triggers our own shame
- **Perfectionism protects against shame** but creates more shame when standards aren't met
- **Shame resilience requires** normalizing imperfection and separating behavior from identity
- **Repair is more important than perfection**—owning and fixing shame responses models resilience
- **Children need to see parents** being self-compassionate to learn they're lovable as-is
- **Breaking shame cycles happens** through daily choices of compassion over criticism

The journey from shame to self-compassion isn't linear. You'll have days when the critic wins, when old patterns resurface, when you pass on what you're trying to heal. But each moment of awareness, each choice of kindness, each repaired rupture weakens shame's hold on your family line. In our next chapter, we'll explore what happens when the fear isn't about being defective but about failing—when every mistake feels like proof of inevitable defeat.

Chapter 5: When Success Never Feels Enough - The Failure Schema

"You Can Do Better" - The Achievement Trap

David's hands shook as he gripped his daughter's report card. B+ in Advanced Placement Chemistry. His chest tightened, vision blurred at the edges—classic panic attack symptoms he knew well. But this wasn't about a presentation at work or a performance review. This was about a sixteen-year-old's grade that most parents would celebrate.

"B plus," he managed to say, his voice carrying decades of disappointment. "What happened?"

His daughter's shoulders sagged. She'd studied for weeks, given up social events, pushed herself to exhaustion. But in David's world—shaped by a failure schema that whispered "nothing is ever enough"—a B+ was evidence of inadequacy. His inadequacy as a parent. Her inadequacy as a student. Their shared destiny of falling short.

"I tried my best, Dad," she said quietly.

"Your best should be better," he replied, echoing words his own father had branded into his psyche forty years earlier. The cycle spun forward, another generation learning that their worth was measured in achievements that would never be enough.

How Fear of Failure Creates Anxious Achievers

The failure schema doesn't create lazy children—it creates anxious ones. Children who lie awake reviewing their day for mistakes, who melt down over minor errors, who measure their worth in gold stars and test scores. These children aren't motivated by joy in learning or pride in growth. They're driven by terror of disappointing the parent whose love feels conditional on performance[17].

This schema manifests as:

- **Chronic anxiety** about performance
- **Perfectionism** that paralyzes rather than motivates
- **Fear of trying** new things (might fail)
- **Identity fusion** with achievements
- **Imposter syndrome** starting in childhood
- **Burnout** before they even reach adulthood

Research on achievement pressure shows alarming rates of anxiety and depression among high-achieving students[18]. These aren't children celebrating their successes—they're children who can't enjoy achievements because they're already worried about the next challenge, the next opportunity to fail, the next confirmation that they're not enough.

Lisa watched her eight-year-old son practice piano, his small fingers stumbling over a difficult passage. With each mistake, his frustration grew. "I can't do it!" he finally exploded, slamming his hands on the keys. "I'm stupid at this!"

She recognized her own voice in his self-attack. The failure schema teaching another generation that struggle equals inadequacy, that anything less than immediate mastery means deficiency.

The Difference Between Encouragement and Pressure

Many parents with failure schemas believe they're being encouraging when they're actually applying pressure. They can't see the difference because their own parents called pressure "believing in your potential" or "wanting the best for you." Understanding this distinction is crucial:

Encouragement sounds like:

- "I see how hard you're working"
- "What did you learn from this?"
- "Your effort is paying off"
- "Mistakes help us grow"
- "I'm proud of your courage to try"

Pressure sounds like:

- "You can do better than this"
- "I expect more from you"
- "Don't disappoint me"
- "Failure isn't an option"
- "You need to be the best"

Encouragement focuses on process, effort, and growth. Pressure focuses on outcomes, comparisons, and meeting expectations. Encouragement builds resilience. Pressure builds anxiety.

Consider these two responses to the same situation:

Child gets second place in science fair

Pressure Response: "Second place? What did the winner do that you didn't? Next year you need to work harder. I know you can win if you really apply yourself."

Encouragement Response: "You worked so hard on your project! Tell me what you learned. How do you feel about what you accomplished?"

One response teaches that second place equals failure. The other celebrates growth and learning.

Why Some Parents Live Through Their Children

The failure schema creates a specific kind of enmeshment where parents' self-worth becomes entangled with their children's achievements. Every report card becomes a judgment on parenting. Every sports game determines family worth. Every college acceptance or rejection letter decides whether the parent succeeded or failed.

This happens because:

- Parents never resolved their own achievement wounds
- Self-worth remains externally determined
- Childhood messages about conditional love persist
- Fear of judgment from others dominates
- Identity beyond achievement was never developed

David's panic over the B+ wasn't really about his daughter's chemistry grade. It was about his father's voice: "Davids don't settle for second best." It was about being pulled from Little League for striking out, denied dessert for A-minus grades, told he'd "never amount to anything" when he chose teaching over law school.

Now his daughter's achievements had become his report card as a parent. Her success proved he wasn't the failure his father predicted. Her struggles confirmed his deepest fear—that failure was genetic, inherited, inevitable.

Creating Intrinsic vs. Extrinsic Motivation

Children need to develop internal drivers for growth rather than external fear of failure. The research on motivation is clear: extrinsic motivation (rewards, punishments, parental approval) creates compliance but kills creativity, joy, and genuine engagement[19]. Intrinsic motivation (curiosity, mastery, purpose) creates lifelong learners who can weather setbacks.

Extrinsic Motivation looks like:

- Doing homework to avoid punishment
- Studying to please parents
- Playing sports for trophies
- Choosing activities based on college applications
- Measuring worth by external validation

Intrinsic Motivation looks like:

- Reading because stories fascinate
- Practicing skills to improve
- Playing sports for joy and friendship
- Pursuing genuine interests
- Finding satisfaction in growth itself

The shift from extrinsic to intrinsic requires parents to:

1. Stop tying love to achievement
2. Celebrate effort over outcome
3. Allow children to choose some activities
4. Model learning for joy
5. Share your own struggles and growth

Case Studies in Failure Schema

Case Study 1: David's Panic Pattern David grew up in a family where second place meant first loser. His father, a successful businessman, measured everything in wins and losses. David's childhood was a series of competitions he could never quite win. Even when he succeeded—valedictorian, full scholarship, medical degree—his father found flaws. "Why not Harvard? Why not chief of surgery?"

Now David's daughter was living under the same microscope. He tracked her grades obsessively, hired tutors at the first sign of struggle, scheduled her life around achievement. When she got the B+ in chemistry, he didn't just see a grade—he saw his father's disappointed face, his own inadequacy reflected back.

The breaking point came when his daughter was hospitalized for exhaustion and malnutrition. She'd been hiding energy drinks under her bed, staying up all night studying, making herself sick with stress. The doctor's words hit hard: "Your daughter is showing signs of severe anxiety and burnout. She's sixteen."

In family therapy, David had to confront how his unhealed wounds were wounding his daughter. He learned to separate her achievements from his worth, to celebrate her effort rather than demanding outcomes, to see that his love had become a prize she could never quite win.

Case Study 2: Lisa's Avoidance Strategy Lisa took the opposite approach—she avoided any activity where her children might not excel. If her son struggled with reading, they'd focus on math. If her daughter wasn't athletic, no sports. Life became a careful dance around potential failure.

But this protection created its own problems. Her children never learned to struggle, persist, or overcome. They developed fragility around challenges, anxiety about trying new things, and a deep belief that they should only do what came easily.

The pattern revealed itself during a family camping trip. Both children melted down when faced with setting up tents, building fires, hiking uphill—anything that required effort without guaranteed success. Lisa realized her protection had become a prison. Her children were afraid of the very experiences that build resilience.

She began introducing "failure practice"—deliberately trying things they weren't good at. Cooking disasters became family jokes. Art projects that looked nothing like the Pinterest photos were celebrated. Slowly, the family learned that failure wasn't catastrophic but instructive.

Case Study 3: The Recovering Achievement Family The Patel family looked successful from outside—two doctor parents, children in gifted programs, walls covered in certificates and trophies. But inside, everyone was exhausted, anxious, and desperately unhappy.

It started unraveling when their eldest, Priya, was rejected from her dream college despite perfect grades. She didn't just cry— she collapsed. "I did everything right," she sobbed. "I gave up everything. What was it all for?"

Her parents, Raj and Anita, saw their own childhoods reflected in her despair. They'd both been pushed relentlessly, achieved greatly, and felt empty. Success hadn't brought happiness, just more pressure to maintain it.

The family entered therapy together, working to redefine success. They created new family values: curiosity over achievement, effort over outcome, wellbeing over winning. Raj started sharing his medical school failures. Anita talked about career doubts. Priya took a gap year to discover what she actually wanted.

The younger children watched this transformation with initial confusion, then relief. The twelve-year-old quit violin (which he hated) to try theater. The ten-year-old started bringing home art instead of just perfect math tests. The family learned to celebrate growth, creativity, and joy—foreign concepts in their achievement-obsessed world.

Practical Exercises

Values Clarification for Your Family

Sit together and explore what really matters:

1. **Individual Values**: Each person lists their top 5 values

2. **Family Discussion**: Share lists without judgment
3. **Common Ground**: Find shared values
4. **Reality Check**: How do current activities align with values?
5. **Adjustment**: What needs to change?

Common discoveries:

- "Success" isn't actually on anyone's list
- Connection, joy, and growth matter more
- Many activities serve ego, not values
- Time allocation doesn't match priorities

Effort vs. Outcome Praise Practice

Transform your response patterns:

Outcome Praise: "You got an A! You're so smart!" *Effort Praise*: "You worked really hard to understand that material!"

Outcome Praise: "You won the game! You're the best!" *Effort Praise*: "You kept trying even when they were ahead. That took courage!"

Outcome Praise: "Your painting is beautiful!" *Effort Praise*: "I can see you experimented with new colors. Tell me about your choices!"

Creating Failure-Safe Zones

Designate times and spaces where failure is celebrated:

- **Failure Friday**: Share the week's mistakes and learnings
- **Experiment Hour**: Try something new without expectation
- **Mistake Museum**: Display failed attempts with pride
- **Story Time**: Parents share their own failure stories

- **Growth Garden**: Track progress, not perfection

Redefining Family Success Metrics

Move beyond grades and trophies:

Old Metrics:

- GPA rankings
- Sports victories
- Award counts
- College admissions
- Salary potential

New Metrics:

- Problems solved creatively
- Kindness shown
- Resilience demonstrated
- Joy experienced
- Growth achieved

Developing Growth Mindset Activities

Based on Carol Dweck's research[20], practice reframing:

Fixed Mindset: "I'm not good at math" *Growth Mindset*: "I'm learning math step by step"

Fixed Mindset: "I failed" *Growth Mindset*: "I haven't succeeded yet"

Fixed Mindset: "This is too hard" *Growth Mindset*: "This will help me grow"

Parent-Child Interaction Examples

Post-Game Conversations (Win or Lose)

After a Loss:

Failure Schema Response: "What went wrong out there? You need to practice harder. I'm disappointed in how you played. The other team wanted it more."

Healthy Response: "How are you feeling? What was challenging today? I saw you support your teammate when they missed—that was great sportsmanship. What did you enjoy about playing?"

After a Win:

Failure Schema Response: "Good, but you could have scored more. Don't get complacent. Next week's team is better. You can't let up now."

Healthy Response: "How did it feel to play well together? What worked for your team today? I loved watching you have fun out there!"

Homework Help Without Hovering

Child Struggling with Assignment:

Failure Schema Response: [Takes over] "Here, let me do it. You're doing it wrong. This is simple—why can't you get it? We need to get this perfect."

Healthy Response: "This looks challenging. What part are you working on? Would it help to talk through your thinking? I'm here if you need me, but I know you can figure this out."

Celebrating Learning from Mistakes

Child Makes Error on Test:

Failure Schema Response: "How did you miss this? We went over it! This is careless. You're smarter than this. What will your teacher think?"

Healthy Response: "Mistakes show us what to practice next. What do you understand now that you didn't before? Everyone makes errors—that's how we learn!"

Healing Strategies

Examining Your Worth Beyond Achievement

Questions for reflection:

- Who are you when you're not achieving?
- What did you love before it became competitive?
- If no one was watching or measuring, what would you do?
- What brings joy without external validation?
- Who loves you for being, not doing?

Healing Your Own Failure Wounds

1. **Timeline Your Achievement Pressure**: When did it start? Who delivered messages?
2. **Grieve Lost Childhood**: What did you sacrifice for success?
3. **Challenge Old Messages**: Are they true? Are they helpful?
4. **Find Achievement-Free Zones**: Hobbies with no measurement
5. **Practice Self-Compassion**: You are enough as you are

Finding Intrinsic Motivation

Rediscover what drives you internally:

- What fascinates you?
- What would you do for free?
- When do you lose track of time?
- What problems do you want to solve?
- What legacy matters to you?

Model this discovery for your children.

Prevention for Children

Teaching Resilience Through Failure

Resilience isn't avoiding failure—it's recovering from it:

1. **Normalize Struggle**: "This is hard, and hard is okay"
2. **Process Together**: "What did this teach us?"
3. **Problem-Solve**: "What could we try next?"
4. **Celebrate Courage**: "You tried something scary!"
5. **Share Stories**: Your own failures and recoveries

Building Competence Gradually

- Start with small challenges
- Increase difficulty slowly
- Allow genuine struggle
- Resist rescue urges
- Celebrate incremental progress

Fostering Internal Motivation

- Ask "What interests you?" not "What are you good at?"
- Allow quitting activities they don't enjoy
- Create space for unstructured exploration
- Value questions over answers
- Model learning for joy

A New Definition of Success

David now celebrates his daughter's curiosity more than her grades. She's exploring chemistry because she loves it, not because she needs another A. Lisa's children try new things with enthusiasm rather than anxiety, knowing failure is just information. The Patel family has redefined success as growth, connection, and wellbeing rather than achievement at any cost.

Your failure schema whispers lies about worth being earned, love being conditional, and achievement being salvation. But your children need to know they're valuable simply for existing. They need to see you fail and recover, struggle and persist, choose joy over achievement.

Every time you celebrate effort over outcome, every time you share your own struggles, every time you choose connection over competition, you're breaking the achievement trap. Your children can achieve greatly when they're not afraid to fail—when they know their worth isn't measured in medals but in their willingness to grow.

The next chapter explores what happens when all these schemas intersect, when parents must navigate multiple patterns while building something new. But for now, practice failing at something today. Let your children see you struggle, laugh, and try again. Show them that success isn't about never falling—it's about making failure your teacher rather than your identity.

Key Takeaways

- **Fear of failure creates anxious achievers** who measure worth through external validation
- **Pressure masquerades as encouragement** but focuses on outcomes rather than growth
- **Parents living through children's achievements** haven't resolved their own worth issues

- **Intrinsic motivation develops** when children pursue interests for joy, not approval
- **Failure schemas transmit** through criticism of mistakes and conditional love
- **Resilience requires experiencing failure** in safe environments with supportive responses
- **Redefining success** as growth, effort, and wellbeing breaks generational achievement traps

Chapter 6: The Lighthouse Parent - Integration and Balance

"Being the Parent You Needed"

The lighthouse stands firm against crashing waves, its beam cutting through darkness—not controlling the ships, just illuminating the way. This is what Rachel finally understood after years of swinging between her schemas like a pendulum. Some days her abandonment fears made her cling too tightly. Other days her mistrust had her building walls. But that Tuesday evening, watching her children play while she prepared dinner, something shifted.

"Mom, can I go to Jake's house?" her ten-year-old asked.

Every schema fired at once. Abandonment whispered he was choosing friends over family. Mistrust questioned Jake's parents' supervision. Failure suggested she should be enough entertainment. But Rachel had learned something new—she could feel all these old patterns without being controlled by them.

"Tell me about the plan," she said calmly, buying time to breathe through the schema storm. She was becoming what her family needed: a lighthouse parent. Steady. Present. Illuminating without controlling.

Integrating Healing Across All Schemas

Most parents don't have just one schema—they have several that take turns running the show. Monday's abandonment fears become Tuesday's emotional shutdown become Wednesday's shame spiral. The exhaustion comes not just from each schema but from the constant switching between them[21].

Integration means learning to:

- **Recognize multiple schemas** operating simultaneously
- **Understand how schemas interact** and trigger each other
- **Develop a unified response** rather than reactive swings
- **Create consistent family patterns** despite internal chaos
- **Build a coherent narrative** from fragmented experiences

Think of schemas like different radio stations playing in your head. Sometimes they overlap, creating static. Sometimes one drowns out the others. Integration is learning to tune into what your children actually need rather than what your schemas are broadcasting.

Rachel discovered her schemas often worked in sequence. Her son wanting independence (abandonment trigger) led to interrogating him about friends (mistrust activation) which ended with her feeling like a failure as a mother (failure schema). Once she mapped this pattern, she could interrupt it.

The Lighthouse Parenting Model

Lighthouse parenting offers a middle path between the extremes schemas create[22]. Unlike helicopter parents (hovering anxiously) or submarine parents (surfacing rarely), lighthouse parents provide:

Consistent Presence Without Intrusion

- Available when needed
- Not constantly intervening
- Visible and reliable
- Respecting children's autonomy

Illumination Without Control

- Sharing wisdom when asked
- Highlighting dangers without panic
- Offering perspective not commands
- Trusting children to navigate

Steady Beam Despite Internal Weather

- Maintaining consistency despite triggers
- Same rules regardless of schema activation
- Predictable responses children can count on
- Emotional regulation modeled daily

The lighthouse doesn't chase ships or build walls around them. It simply stands firm, shining light, letting each vessel find its way.

Creating Secure Attachment While Healing

Here's the paradox: you're learning secure attachment while teaching it. You're building the plane while flying it. This is the reality of schema-informed parenting—healing happens in real time, with real children who need you now[23].

Secure attachment doesn't require perfect parents. It requires:

1. **Rupture and Repair**: Messing up and making it right
2. **Good Enough Consistency**: Not perfect, just reliable
3. **Emotional Availability**: Present even when uncomfortable
4. **Reflective Functioning**: Understanding your child's inner world
5. **Coherent Narrative**: Making sense of your story to help them write theirs

The Williams family demonstrated this beautifully. Both parents had significant schemas, yet their children were developing secure attachment. How? Through what they called "real-time repair."

When Mom's abandonment schema made her panic about a sleepover, she'd say: "I'm feeling worried because of my own stuff, not because of you. Let me take a breath and try again." When Dad's emotional deprivation made him shut down during homework struggles, he'd return later: "I went blank when you were upset. That's my challenge, not yours. Can we talk now?"

The children learned that parents were human, feelings were manageable, and relationships could handle imperfection.

When Different Schemas Conflict

The real complexity comes when multiple schemas activate simultaneously, creating internal gridlock. Rachel faced this constantly:

- Abandonment schema said: "Keep them close"
- Mistrust schema said: "Don't let anyone near"
- Emotional deprivation said: "Don't feel this"
- Failure schema said: "You're doing it all wrong"

The schemas created impossible equations. How do you keep children close while trusting others? How do you connect emotionally while feeling defective? These internal conflicts create the inconsistency that confuses children.

The solution isn't choosing one schema over another—it's finding the wisdom buried in each while rejecting the extremes:

- From abandonment: Value connection without suffocating
- From mistrust: Maintain appropriate caution without paranoia

- From emotional deprivation: Appreciate stability without emptiness
- From defectiveness: Strive for growth without perfectionism
- From failure: Encourage achievement without pressure

Case Study: The Chen Family's Integration Journey

The Chen family came to therapy in chaos. Mom (Lisa) had severe abandonment and emotional deprivation schemas. Dad (James) carried mistrust and failure schemas. Their three children were showing signs of all these patterns—anxious attachment, social withdrawal, perfectionism.

Their schemas created a perfect storm. Lisa's abandonment fears made her hover, which triggered James's need for control. His mistrust of others limited social opportunities, which increased her emotional isolation. Their combined failure schemas created unbearable pressure on the children to be perfect.

The breakthrough came through "schema mapping" as a family. They literally drew their patterns on a large paper:

- Lisa's abandonment arrows pointing inward (pulling close)
- James's mistrust arrows pointing outward (pushing away)
- Children caught in the crossfire of opposing forces

Seeing it visually helped them understand the family dynamics. They began creating "integration practices":

Morning Integration: Each parent did a schema check before breakfast. "What's loud today? What does my family need from me?"

Evening Debrief: Parents met for 10 minutes after bedtime to discuss schema activations and plan repairs.

Weekly Family Meeting: Everyone shared their struggles and successes with patterns.

Schema Interruption Signal: Anyone could make a "T" with their hands for "time-out" when they noticed schemas taking over.

Six months later, the family had transformed. Not perfect—Lisa still panicked sometimes, James still withdrew. But they had a shared language, mutual understanding, and tools for integration. The children were developing their own awareness: "Mom, is this your abandonment talking?" became a gentle family joke that interrupted patterns with compassion.

Creating Your Family Mission Statement

A family mission statement becomes your lighthouse—a fixed point when schemas create storm. The process:

Step 1: Individual Reflection Each family member (age-appropriate) answers:

- What kind of family do I want?
- What values matter most?
- How do I want to feel at home?
- What do I want to give and receive?

Step 2: Family Sharing Without judgment, each person shares their answers. Notice themes.

Step 3: Finding Common Ground What do everyone's answers share? Safety? Fun? Growth? Connection?

Step 4: Drafting Together Create a simple statement everyone understands and remembers.

Step 5: Living Document Review monthly, adjust as needed, use during conflicts.

The Chen family's mission statement: "We are a family that learns together, loves imperfectly, and always makes room for repair."

Simple. Clear. Revolutionary for a family drowning in schemas.

Practical Tools

Daily Schema Check-In Practice

Create a morning routine for parents:

1. **Body Scan**: Where do I feel tension? What schema lives there?
2. **Emotion Check**: What am I feeling? Which schema is it feeding?
3. **Need Assessment**: What does my schema want? What do my children need?
4. **Integration Intention**: How will I respond from wisdom, not wounds?
5. **Anchor Phrase**: Choose a mantra for the day ("I am the lighthouse")

Family Regulation Routines

Build predictable patterns that regulate everyone:

Morning Rhythm:

- Same wake time
- Connection before correction
- Breakfast together when possible
- Launch with encouragement

After School/Work Transition:

- 10 minutes to decompress
- Share one good thing
- Address needs before tasks
- Snack and connection

Evening Wind-Down:

- Technology boundaries
- Calming activities
- Individual check-ins
- Gratitude practice

Bedtime Consistency:

- Same routine nightly
- Connection rituals
- Tomorrow's preview
- Words of affirmation

Building Your Parenting Support Team

Lighthouse parents need their own lighthouses:

1. **Schema-Aware Friend**: Someone who understands your patterns
2. **Professional Support**: Therapist familiar with schema work
3. **Partner Alliance**: Regular check-ins about patterns
4. **Extended Family Allies**: Those who support your healing
5. **Parent Groups**: Others on similar journeys

Rachel created her "lighthouse council"—three friends who met monthly for dinner. They knew each other's schemas, called out patterns gently, celebrated progress. No judgment, just witnesses to the work.

The Integration Path Forward

Becoming a lighthouse parent doesn't mean your schemas disappear. Rachel still feels the pull of abandonment, the whisper of mistrust. But now she recognizes these as weather patterns, not her identity. She stands firm, beam steady, while storms pass through.

Your children don't need you to be schema-free. They need you to be aware, working on integration, showing them that healing is possible. Every time you catch yourself mid-schema and choose differently, you're teaching them that patterns can change. Every repair shows them relationships can handle truth. Every integrated response proves that wisdom is stronger than wounds.

The lighthouse doesn't fight the storm or pretend calm seas. It simply stands, shines, and guides ships home. This is your calling—not perfection, but presence. Not being healed, but healing. Not having arrived, but showing the way.

Chapter 7: Partners in Healing - When Parents Have Different Schemas

"Your Trauma Meets My Trauma"

Sarah was building walls while Mike was tearing them down. Their kitchen had become a battlefield where invisible schemas waged war through parenting decisions. "She needs to learn independence!" Mike insisted about their clingy six-year-old. His mistrust schema couldn't tolerate neediness—it felt dangerous, weak, something that predators exploited.

"She needs to know we're here for her!" Sarah shot back, her abandonment schema in overdrive. The thought of pushing their daughter away felt like creating the very wound she'd spent thirty years trying to heal.

Their daughter stood between them, absorbing the confusion of contradictory messages. Be independent but don't leave. Trust yourself but need us. Grow up but stay close. Two parents, two traumas, one very confused child.

How Different Schemas Interact in Co-Parenting

When two people with different schemas parent together, they create what researchers call "schema dynamics"—predictable patterns of interaction that can either heal or harm[24]. These dynamics include:

Trigger Cascades: One parent's behavior activates the other's schema

- Abandonment parent's clinging triggers mistrust parent's withdrawal
- Emotional deprivation parent's distance triggers failure parent's overcompensation

- Defectiveness parent's criticism triggers abandonment parent's panic

Compensation Battles: Each parent overcompensates for the other

- "You're too soft, so I'll be harder"
- "You're too distant, so I'll be closer"
- "You're too critical, so I'll praise everything"

Schema Polarization: Parents become extreme opposites

- One becomes sergeant, other becomes pushover
- One hovers constantly, other barely engages
- One demands perfection, other accepts anything

Projection Confusion: Each parent sees their schema in the child

- "She's anxious like you" (when child is normal)
- "He's withdrawn like you" (when child is tired)
- "They're failing because of your pressure" (when struggling is typical)

Mike and Sarah demonstrated all these patterns. His mistrust made him see her attachment as weakness. Her abandonment made her see his boundaries as rejection. They were fighting their own childhoods through their child.

Creating Shared Parenting Approaches

The path forward requires moving from "my way versus your way" to "our way." This isn't compromise where everyone loses—it's integration where wisdom emerges. The process involves:

Step 1: Schema Awareness Together Both parents must understand:

- Their own schemas and triggers
- Their partner's schemas and triggers
- How schemas interact dynamically
- Impact on children

Step 2: Finding the Middle Path Between extremes lies wisdom:

- Between clinging and rejecting: secure attachment
- Between suspicion and naiveté: appropriate caution
- Between criticism and permissiveness: supportive guidance
- Between enmeshment and distance: healthy boundaries

Step 3: Creating United Practices Develop specific approaches you both can implement:

- Bedtime routines honoring both needs
- Discipline strategies avoiding both extremes
- Social situations balancing freedom and safety
- Academic expectations merging support with growth

Step 4: Regular Calibration Weekly meetings to:

- Review what worked/didn't work
- Identify schema activations
- Plan repairs if needed
- Adjust strategies together

Supporting Each Other's Healing

Co-parents can be each other's greatest healers or deepest triggers. The difference lies in approach. Healing-focused partners:

Recognize Schema Moments: "I think your abandonment might be activated right now. What do you need?"

Offer Gentle Reality Checks: "Our daughter seems okay. Might this be more about your childhood?"

Create Safety for Vulnerability: "Tell me what you're really afraid of. I won't judge."

Celebrate Progress: "I noticed you stayed calm when she wanted space. That was huge."

Share the Work: "Your mistrust is up today. Want me to handle the playdate discussion?"

The Johnsons mastered this mutual support. When Anna's emotional deprivation made her freeze during their son's tantrum, Paul would step in: "I've got this. Take a break." When Paul's failure schema activated over homework, Anna would intervene: "Let's make this about learning, not grades."

They became each other's schema spotters, not critics but companions in healing.

United Front vs. Authentic Differences

Children need consistency, but not fake uniformity. The goal isn't pretending you agree on everything—it's handling disagreement constructively. There's a difference between:

Destructive Disagreement:

- Fighting in front of children
- Undermining each other
- Using children as messengers
- Making children choose sides

Constructive Difference:

- Acknowledging different perspectives calmly
- Finding common ground publicly
- Discussing major differences privately
- Showing respectful negotiation

The Martinez family modeled this beautifully. When Dad (abandonment) wanted their teen to text constantly during a school trip and Mom (failure) wanted to encourage independence, they handled it skillfully:

To their teen: "Mom and I have different comfort levels about communication. We both want you safe and growing. Let's find something that works for everyone."

They negotiated openly but respectfully, showing their teen that differences can be resolved without drama.

Case Studies: Schema Combination Navigation

Case Study 1: Abandonment Meets Mistrust Emma (abandonment) and Chris (mistrust) created a paradoxical dynamic. She wanted their children close but safe, which meant trusting others for childcare. He wanted them independent but protected, which meant limiting social exposure. Their schemas created impossible equations.

Their eight-year-old daughter developed severe social anxiety, afraid to leave (mom's fear) and afraid to connect (dad's fear). Their five-year-old son rebelled against both, becoming recklessly independent.

Therapy revealed how each parent's solution triggered the other's problem. Emma's clinging made Chris more suspicious of her "weakness." Chris's walls made Emma more desperate for connection. They were in a schema spiral, pulling their children down with them.

The breakthrough: They learned to "schema swap" perspectives. Emma would ask, "What would healthy caution look like here?" Chris would ask, "What would secure connection look like?" They found middle ground:

- Gradual social expansion with vetted families
- Independence practices within safe boundaries
- Connection rituals that didn't suffocate
- Trust-building exercises for the whole family

Case Study 2: Emotional Deprivation Meets Failure David (emotional deprivation) and Patricia (failure) created a family of high achievement and emotional emptiness. He couldn't provide emotional support. She compensated by pushing for external success. Their children excelled at everything except feeling.

Their teenage son was accepted to elite universities but couldn't name a single emotion. Their daughter won every award but cut herself in secret. Success without soul was killing their family.

The work began with David learning basic emotional literacy—literally using feeling wheels and emotion cards like a foreign language student. Patricia had to grieve that achievement wouldn't heal her husband's emotional absence or her own worth wounds.

Together they created "Feeling Fridays"—family time with no achievement talk allowed. Just emotions, connections, presence. It was awkward, like learning to walk again. But slowly, the family developed a new language beyond grades and goals.

Case Study 3: Multiple Schema Chaos The Thompson family represented schema chaos. Mom carried abandonment and defectiveness. Dad held mistrust and emotional deprivation.

Their three children were developing their own schema combinations in response.

Family life was exhausting. Every decision triggered multiple schemas. Bedtime activated four different patterns. School events created schema storms. They were drowning in their own patterns.

Their therapist introduced "schema rounds"—each parent would name their activated schema before discussing any parenting decision. "My abandonment is scared she'll feel rejected." "My mistrust wonders about that coach." Just naming schemas reduced their power.

They created a visual schema map for their refrigerator. When patterns activated, family members could point instead of argue. Children learned to say, "Dad, is that your mistrust or real danger?" with genuine curiosity, not judgment.

The family developed "schema-free zones"—activities where patterns weren't allowed to drive decisions. Game night. Saturday morning pancakes. Beach walks. These became sacred spaces for just being together.

Practical Exercises

Schema Mapping for Couples

Create a visual map together:

1. **Individual Maps**: Each partner draws their schemas as shapes/colors
2. **Overlay Maps**: Put them together, notice overlaps and conflicts
3. **Interaction Arrows**: Draw how schemas trigger each other

4. **Impact on Children**: Add how dynamics affect each child
5. **Integration Vision**: Create new map of balanced responses

Co-Regulation Techniques for Parents

When one parent is schema-activated:

The STOP Protocol:

- **S**ee the schema: "I notice your abandonment is activated"
- **T**ake space: "Let's pause for five minutes"
- **O**ffer support: "What do you need right now?"
- **P**lan together: "How should we handle this?"

Physical Co-Regulation:

- Stand side by side, not face to face
- Match breathing rhythms
- Light touch if welcomed
- Walk together while talking

Verbal Co-Regulation:

- "We're on the same team"
- "Your schema makes sense given your history"
- "Our child is okay, we're okay"
- "Let's find our middle ground"

Conflict Resolution When Schemas Clash

The HEAL framework:

Halt the escalation: Recognize schemas are driving conflict
Explore underlying needs: What is each schema trying to

protect? **A**lign on child's needs: What does our child actually need? **L**ink new response: How can we meet everyone's needs?

Example:

- Halt: "We're both triggered. Let's breathe."
- Explore: "You need her close. I need her strong."
- Align: "She needs both connection and confidence."
- Link: "Let's practice short separations with warm returns."

Creating Complementary Parenting Strategies

Turn schema differences into strengths:

Abandonment + Mistrust:

- Abandonment parent handles emotional connection
- Mistrust parent teaches appropriate boundaries
- Together: Secure attachment with good judgment

Emotional Deprivation + Failure:

- Emotional deprivation parent provides stability
- Failure parent encourages growth
- Together: Steady support for development

Defectiveness + Abandonment:

- Defectiveness parent notices areas for growth
- Abandonment parent ensures unconditional love
- Together: Growth within security

Building a Schema-Informed Partnership

Mike and Sarah now see their kitchen conversations differently. When schemas activate, they name them: "My mistrust is worried about that family." "My abandonment is panicking about independence." They've learned to pause, breathe, find wisdom between extremes.

Their daughter no longer stands confused between them. She sees parents working together, different but aligned, healing while parenting. She's learning that people can have different experiences and still love each other, that repair is possible, that families can hold multiple truths.

Your partnership doesn't require identical schemas or perfect healing. It requires recognition that you're both doing your best with the patterns you inherited. Every time you choose curiosity over judgment, every time you find middle ground, every time you support each other's healing while parenting together— you're creating new possibility.

Two lighthouses can illuminate more ocean than one. Your different perspectives, when integrated rather than battled, provide your children with a fuller view of healthy relationship. Show them that differences can dance together, that healing happens in partnership, that love is bigger than schemas.

Takeaways:

- **Different schemas create predictable dynamics** that can escalate or heal depending on awareness
- **Shared parenting approaches emerge** from finding middle ground between extremes
- **Partners can be healers or triggers**—the difference is conscious support versus reactive criticism
- **Children need consistency not uniformity**—show them respectful negotiation of differences
- **Schema mapping reveals family dynamics** and creates shared language for healing
- **Complementary strategies** turn schema differences into family strengths

The journey continues as you learn to stand firm while storms pass, to shine steadily despite internal weather, to guide without controlling. In the chapters ahead, we'll explore how schemas manifest differently across developmental stages and how extended family and community play roles in breaking generational patterns. But for now, practice being the lighthouse—present, steady, illuminating the way home.

Chapter 8: Age-Appropriate Healing - Developmental Considerations

"Right Support, Right Time"

The same schema looks completely different in a toddler's tantrum than in a teenager's silence. Maria learned this the hard way when her proven strategies for her eight-year-old suddenly failed with her now-thirteen-year-old daughter. The abandonment fears that once showed up as bedtime clinginess had morphed into explosive anger whenever Maria showed concern.

"You're suffocating me!" her daughter screamed, slamming her bedroom door. The words hit Maria like physical blows. She'd spent five years learning to manage her abandonment schema, creating secure routines, mastering the balance between connection and space. But puberty had changed all the rules.

What Maria hadn't understood—what many parents miss—is that schemas aren't static. They shape-shift with development, finding new ways to express old wounds. The work of schema-informed parenting must grow and adapt as our children do.

How Schemas Manifest at Different Developmental Stages

Each developmental stage offers unique challenges and opportunities for schema healing. The infant who fusses at separation becomes the toddler who tantrums at transitions becomes the teenager who rages at boundaries. Same schema, different costume[25].

Understanding these manifestations helps you:

- **Recognize schemas** beneath age-typical behaviors

- **Differentiate** between development and dysfunction
- **Adapt your responses** to meet changing needs
- **Prevent schemas** from solidifying at each stage
- **Support healing** in developmentally appropriate ways

Think of development as a river. Your schemas are rocks in that river. At different points, the water flows differently around those same rocks—sometimes creating gentle eddies, sometimes dangerous rapids. Your job is to help your child navigate each stretch of river, knowing where your rocks create turbulence.

Adjusting Your Approach as Children Grow

What soothes a four-year-old may insult a fourteen-year-old. What terrifies a toddler may thrill a teen. Schema-informed parenting requires constant recalibration, staying attuned not just to your patterns but to your child's developmental needs.

The adjustment involves:

Language Evolution: From "Mommy always comes back" to "I trust your judgment" **Physical Distance**: From constant touch to respecting personal space **Emotional Availability**: From immediate soothing to patient witnessing **Control Balance**: From protective limits to collaborative boundaries **Independence Support**: From supervised exploration to genuine autonomy

The Patel family discovered this when their abandonment-schema responses backfired with their teenage son. The location tracking, constant check-ins, and emotional interrogations that had felt like love to him at eight now felt like prison at fifteen. They had to learn a new dance—one where love meant letting go, not holding tight.

Teen Schemas vs. Childhood Schemas

Adolescence adds complexity to schema work. Teenagers aren't just dealing with inherited family patterns—they're developing their own schemas based on peer relationships, first loves, social media, and identity formation. You're now managing:

- **Your schemas** (triggered by their growing independence)
- **Inherited patterns** (what they absorbed from you)
- **Emerging schemas** (from their own experiences)
- **Developmental storms** (normal teen brain chaos)

This creates what I call "schema soup"—a swirling mixture of old patterns, new wounds, hormonal intensity, and identity confusion. Parents must become skilled at distinguishing ingredients:

Is this defiance abandonment fear or normal individuation? Is this perfectionism an inherited failure schema or peer pressure? Is this withdrawal emotional deprivation or introversion? Is this anger a trauma response or teenage frustration?

Supporting Individuation While Healing

The ultimate paradox of parenting: preparing children to leave while healing your fear of being left. Supporting healthy individuation when you have attachment wounds requires extraordinary courage. It means:

Celebrating Distance: "I'm proud you want to handle this yourself" **Tolerating Rejection**: Understanding "I hate you" as "I need space to grow" **Allowing Failure**: Letting them learn from consequences you could prevent **Witnessing Pain**: Not rushing to fix what they need to feel **Trusting Process**: Believing they'll find their way

Age-Specific Guides

Infancy & Toddlerhood (0-3)

At this stage, your schemas primarily affect co-regulation and attachment formation[26]. Infants are emotional sponges, absorbing your nervous system state.

Abandonment Schema Impact:

- Difficulty with sleep training (separation feels dangerous)
- Anxious response to normal infant distress
- Over-monitoring of attachment behaviors
- Panic at developmental independence (crawling away)

Healthy Adaptations:

- Practice brief separations with calm returns
- Narrate permanence: "I'm in the kitchen, you're safe"
- Celebrate exploration: "Look how brave you are!"
- Create predictable routines that build trust

Case Example: Sarah's ten-month-old began crawling toward other adults at playgroup. Her abandonment schema screamed danger—he was choosing others over her. She'd swoop in, redirecting him back. A wise friend noticed: "He explores because he feels secure with you." Sarah learned to sit still, letting him venture out and return, building both their confidence.

Early Childhood (4-7)

This stage brings magical thinking, emotional intensity, and first social wounds. Children are old enough to absorb family patterns but too young to understand them[27].

Mistrust Schema Impact:

- Interrogating about preschool interactions
- Limiting social opportunities
- Transmitting hypervigilance
- Interpreting normal conflicts as betrayal

Healthy Adaptations:

- Teach emotional vocabulary before suspicion
- Practice "checking the facts" together
- Model trusting relationships
- Create safe social experiences

Case Example: David's mistrust activated when his five-year-old said a classmate was "mean." His first instinct: call the school, demand action, consider switching classes. Instead, he paused, asked questions: "What did mean look like? How did you handle it? What help do you need?" His son described a normal playground dispute, already resolved. David's pause prevented schema transmission.

Middle Childhood (8-11)

Children develop complex social awareness, academic pressures, and beginning identity formation. They're sophisticated enough to notice family patterns but still dependent enough to be shaped by them[28].

Failure Schema Impact:

- Academic pressure intensifies
- Extracurricular overload
- Constant performance measurement
- Identity fusion with achievement

Healthy Adaptations:

- Introduce growth mindset explicitly

- Share your own failure stories
- Celebrate effort separately from outcome
- Create achievement-free zones

Case Example: The Chen family's eleven-year-old quit piano after years of lessons. Mom's failure schema activated: "We don't quit! What will people think?" But she caught herself, remembered her own forced violin lessons, the joy they stole. "Tell me about your decision," she said instead. Her daughter explained she wanted to try art. They ceremonially retired the piano books, celebrating years of learning rather than mourning "failure."

Adolescence (12-18)

The most complex stage for schema work. Teenagers need to separate while staying connected, rebel while feeling secure, become themselves while honoring their roots[29].

All Schemas Intensify:

- Abandonment: Teen independence feels like rejection
- Mistrust: Teen privacy feels like betrayal
- Emotional Deprivation: Teen intensity overwhelms
- Defectiveness: Teen struggles confirm worst fears
- Failure: Teen choices threaten family image

Healthy Adaptations:

- Respect developmental need for separation
- Offer connection without requiring it
- Share power in age-appropriate ways
- Focus on safety over control
- Model your own ongoing growth

Case Example: Marcus's sixteen-year-old daughter started dating someone he didn't like. Every schema fired at once.

Abandonment: she's choosing him over family. Mistrust: this boy has ulterior motives. Failure: what if she gets hurt/pregnant/derailed?

Instead of forbidding (which would guarantee rebellion), Marcus said: "Tell me what you like about him. Help me understand." He shared his concerns without attacking, set safety boundaries without controlling, stayed connected through the challenge. When they broke up months later, his daughter came to him for comfort—the door he'd kept open by managing his schemas.

Practical Tools

Developmental Milestone Guides Through Schema Lens

Track not just what children achieve but how schemas might interfere:

Traditional Milestone: "Plays cooperatively by age 4" *Schema-Informed View*:

- Abandonment parent might not allow cooperative play opportunities
- Mistrust parent might hover, preventing natural interaction
- Consider: Is delay developmental or environmental?

Traditional Milestone: "Develops friendships by age 8" *Schema-Informed View*:

- Emotional deprivation family might not model connection
- Defectiveness messages might create social anxiety
- Consider: What friendship skills need teaching?

Age-Appropriate Conversations About Family Patterns

Ages 4-7: Simple, concrete language "Sometimes Mommy worries too much because her mommy worried too much. I'm learning to worry just the right amount."

Ages 8-11: More complex explanations "Our family has patterns passed down through generations. Some help us, some don't. We're working to keep the good ones and change the others."

Ages 12+: Full collaboration "I've noticed I get anxious when you want independence. That's my old stuff, not about you. How can we handle this together?"

Supporting Children's Own Schema Healing

As children recognize inherited patterns, support their healing:

1. **Validate Their Experience**: "Yes, you're right. I do get scared when you pull away."
2. **Take Responsibility**: "That's my pattern to heal, not your job to manage."
3. **Collaborate on Solutions**: "What would help you feel free while I work on this?"
4. **Celebrate Their Awareness**: "I'm proud you can see these patterns."
5. **Model Ongoing Work**: "I'm still learning too. We're doing this together."

Developmental Schema Healing in Action

The Morrison family exemplified age-appropriate healing across four children. Mom's abandonment schema and Dad's failure schema affected each child differently:

- The 3-year-old needed consistent routines and separation practice
- The 7-year-old needed emotional vocabulary and social support

- The 11-year-old needed achievement pressure relief and identity exploration
- The 15-year-old needed respect for autonomy and collaborative problem-solving

They held monthly family meetings where each child could share (age-appropriately) how family patterns affected them. The teenager led discussions about independence. The middle schooler created feeling charts. The seven-year-old drew pictures of emotions. Even the toddler participated by showing happy/sad faces.

This developmental approach meant no child felt singled out or broken. Everyone was growing, parents included. The patterns became family projects rather than family secrets.

Growing Together Through Time

Maria's thirteen-year-old daughter who slammed doors at perceived suffocation? Six months later, they'd found their new rhythm. Maria learned to offer connection through presence, not probing. Her daughter learned to ask for space without attacking. They developed signals—a raised hand meant "I need distance but still love you."

Schema-informed parenting isn't a one-time fix but a developmental journey. Your four-year-old who needed constant reassurance becomes your fourteen-year-old who needs trusted space. Your schemas remain, but your responses evolve. Every stage offers new chances to heal—both for you and your children.

The beauty lies in growing together. As you adapt your approach to meet their developmental needs, you heal parts of yourself frozen at those same ages. Your teenager's individuation helps you grieve the independence you weren't allowed. Your toddler's tantrums help you honor the emotions you had to suppress. Each stage of their growth offers a stage of your healing.

Chapter 8 Takeaways:

- **Schemas manifest differently** across developmental stages, requiring adapted responses
- **Each stage offers unique opportunities** for both triggering and healing patterns
- **Teen schemas add complexity** as inherited patterns meet new developmental challenges
- **Supporting individuation while healing** abandonment fears requires extraordinary courage
- **Age-appropriate conversations** about patterns help children develop early awareness
- **Developmental healing happens bidirectionally** as children's stages heal parent's frozen parts

Chapter 9: Beyond Nuclear - Extended Family and Community

"It Takes a Village to Break a Pattern"

The doorbell rang, and Jennifer's body went rigid. Thanksgiving had arrived in the form of her mother—the original source of her emotional deprivation schema, now bearing pie and judgment. "Why isn't the house cleaner?" were her first words, followed by, "The children look thin. Are you feeding them properly?"

Jennifer's seven-year-old daughter watched her mother transform—from the warm, present parent they'd been working to become into the shut-down, efficient robot her grandmother expected. Three years of therapy, daily emotional check-ins, and conscious parenting evaporated in the face of the person who'd created the pattern.

This is the challenge no parenting book prepares you for: healing your schemas while surrounded by the people who created them.

Managing Extended Family with Different Schemas

Extended family members often represent "schema headquarters"—the original sources of your patterns. They haven't done the work you have. They see your healing as rejection of family values. They trigger your schemas through:

- **Direct repetition** of old patterns
- **Criticism** of your new approaches
- **Triangulation** with your children
- **Guilt** about changing family traditions
- **Denial** that patterns exist

The complexity multiplies when extended family members have their own untreated schemas interacting with yours. Jennifer's mother's emotional deprivation met her father's failure schema, creating a toxic soup at every gathering. Add aunts with abandonment fears, uncles with mistrust, cousins repeating cycles—family events become schema battlegrounds.

Creating Chosen Family Support

The solution often lies beyond blood relations. Chosen family— friends who understand your healing journey—provide what extended family cannot:

Schema-Aware Support: They recognize your triggers **Healing Partnership**: They're on similar journeys **Safe Practice**: You can try new patterns without judgment **Reality Checking**: They help distinguish past from present **Celebration**: They notice and affirm your growth

The Johnsons created their "Schema Support Squad"—three other families working on generational healing. They met monthly for potlucks where parents could process triggers while kids played. They celebrated schema interruptions like achievements: "I didn't panic when she wanted a sleepover!" "I stayed present during his tantrum!"

These chosen family members became surrogate grandparents, aunts, uncles who modeled healthy patterns. Children saw multiple examples of adults working on growth, normalizing the journey.

When Grandparents Trigger Your Schemas

Grandparents present unique challenges. They're often:

- Primary sources of your schemas
- Beloved by your children despite patterns

- Convinced their methods were/are correct
- Threatened by your different approach
- Capable of undoing your work quickly

Yet they're also family. Children deserve grandparent relationships when safe. The goal becomes harm reduction, not elimination.

Case Study: The Boundaries Dance Michael's father had created his mistrust schema through constant criticism and impossible standards. Now Grandpa did the same to Michael's son: "You throw like a girl. When I was your age..."

Michael's first instinct: cut contact completely. His second: confront aggressively. Neither would help his son. Instead, he created the "Grandpa Protocol":

1. **Pre-visits**: "Grandpa grew up when people thought criticism helped kids. We know better now, but he's still learning."
2. **Real-time interruption**: "Dad, we focus on effort in our family. Jake, show Grandpa your improved form."
3. **Post-visit debrief**: "How did Grandpa's words feel? What's actually true about your throwing?"
4. **Boundary communication**: Private conversation with father about specific limits

It wasn't perfect. Grandpa still criticized. But Michael's son learned to filter messages, keeping connection while rejecting harm.

Building Schema-Informed Community

Beyond family—chosen or biological—lies community. Schools, sports teams, religious organizations, neighborhoods all participate in either perpetuating or healing schemas. Building schema-informed community involves:

Finding Like-Minded People:

- Parenting groups focused on healing
- Therapists who understand intergenerational patterns
- Schools emphasizing emotional development
- Activities promoting growth over achievement

Creating Micro-Communities:

- Start a neighborhood schema support group
- Form partnerships with other healing families
- Share resources and strategies
- Normalize the work of breaking cycles

Educating Existing Communities:

- Talk to teachers about your family's approach
- Share articles with coaches about growth mindset
- Request trauma-informed practices
- Model what you're teaching

Case Studies: Navigating Holidays, Visits, and Boundaries

Case Study 1: The Holiday Survival Plan The Martinez family dreaded Christmas. Extended family meant:

- Grandmother's guilt about their "permissive" parenting
- Uncle's competitiveness triggering failure schemas
- Cousins' achievements paraded for comparison
- Aunt's emotional volatility activating everyone

They created the "Holiday Schema Strategy":

Pre-Holiday Family Meeting: Discussed likely triggers, planned responses, created signals for support needed

Boundary Setting: Shortened visit from five days to two, stayed in hotel not family home, planned breaks

Scripts Ready:

- "We're focusing on effort over grades"
- "Different families have different approaches"
- "Let's change the subject to something positive"

Children Preparation: "Some relatives might say things we don't agree with. You can always check with us about what's true"

Decompression Plan: Built in recovery day after visit, processed experiences together

The shortened visit with clear boundaries transformed the holiday. Not perfect, but manageable.

Case Study 2: The Geographic Solution The Patel family made the difficult decision to relocate away from extended family. Both sets of grandparents lived within ten minutes, dropping by unannounced, undermining parenting decisions, activating schemas daily.

The move wasn't rejection but protection. They:

- Chose distance requiring overnight visits (natural boundaries)
- Controlled frequency and duration of contact
- Created positive visit structures
- Used video calls for regular but bounded connection
- Built new community without schema history

Extended family was furious initially. But over time, the visits became more positive. The grandparents, having to be invited, behaved better as guests. The children maintained relationships without daily schema exposure.

Case Study 3: The Integration Miracle Sometimes extended family surprises you. David's mother had created his emotional deprivation schema through decades of cold efficiency. When she became a grandmother, David maintained strict boundaries, supervising all interactions.

Then his mother asked unexpected questions: "I notice you hug them more than I hugged you. Is that on purpose?" This opened a conversation David never imagined having. His mother revealed her own childhood—wartime trauma, survival requiring emotional shutdown.

Together, three generations began healing. Grandmother learned to say "I love you." David practiced receiving what he'd never gotten. The children witnessed generational healing in real time. Not all families get this gift, but when it happens, the healing accelerates exponentially.

Practical Tools

Scripts for Family Boundaries

For Criticism of Parenting: "We're trying something different with our kids. We'd love your support." "That's interesting perspective. We've found this works better for our family." "Let's agree to disagree on parenting approaches."

For Direct Undermining: "When you contradict our rules, it confuses the children." "We need you to support our decisions even if you disagree." "If you can't respect our boundaries, we'll need to limit visits."

For Schema Activation: "I'm feeling triggered right now and need a break." "That comment brings up old stuff for me. Let's talk later." "I notice we're falling into old patterns. Let's pause."

Creating Support Networks

1. **Identify Needs**: What support would help most?
2. **Search Strategically**: Look for trauma-informed, growth-focused communities
3. **Start Small**: One supportive friend matters more than twenty acquaintances
4. **Be Selective**: Not everyone needs to understand your journey
5. **Reciprocate**: Offer support to others on similar paths

Managing Cultural Expectations

Many cultures emphasize family loyalty that can conflict with schema healing:

- "Family comes first" vs. protecting children from harmful patterns
- "Respect your elders" vs. setting boundaries with parents
- "Don't air dirty laundry" vs. seeking help outside family
- "Blood is thicker" vs. choosing healthier relationships

Navigate by:

- Honoring culture while protecting children
- Finding culturally sensitive therapists
- Connecting with others from similar backgrounds who are healing
- Reframing boundaries as love, not rejection
- Creating new traditions that blend heritage with health

The Extended Network of Healing

Jennifer's mother still criticizes, but Jennifer no longer becomes a robot. She's learned to say, "Mom, I'm working on being more emotionally present with my kids than I learned to be. Would you like to learn with me?" Sometimes her mother softens, sometimes not. But Jennifer's children see her staying true to her values despite pressure.

The village that helps break patterns isn't always the village you're born into. Sometimes you must build it from scratch—friend by friend, family by family, boundary by boundary. Your biological family may never understand your healing journey. But your children need to see you choosing health over habit, growth over tradition when necessary.

Every schema-informed friend you make, every boundary you set with family, every community resource you access creates a stronger foundation for your children. They learn that support exists beyond blood, that chosen family can be just as powerful, that breaking patterns sometimes means breaking ranks.

The ripple effects extend beyond your nuclear family. Other parents watch your boundary-setting and find courage. Extended family members witness your children's emotional health and ask questions. Communities slowly shift as more families prioritize healing over hiding. You become part of the village helping others break their patterns, even as you work on your own.

Key Takeaways

- **Extended family often represents** "schema headquarters" requiring careful boundary management
- **Chosen family provides** crucial support when biological family can't understand healing
- **Grandparents need specific protocols** to maintain connection while preventing schema transmission
- **Schema-informed communities** accelerate healing through shared understanding
- **Cultural expectations** may conflict with healing work, requiring thoughtful navigation
- **The village that breaks patterns** might need to be built rather than inherited

Chapter 10: The Ripple Effect - Raising Cycle-Breakers

"The Generation That Heals"

Eight-year-old Sophia sat in the family meeting, her small voice clear and confident. "Mom, I think your worry is taking over again. Remember what we practiced?" Her mother, Lisa, paused mid-anxiety-spiral about the upcoming school field trip. Her daughter was right. The abandonment schema was driving, not wisdom.

"You're absolutely right, sweetheart. Thank you for catching that. Let me try again."

This moment—a child gently redirecting a parent's schema—represented three generations of healing work. Lisa's grandmother had clung desperately, her mother had alternated between clinging and pushing away, Lisa had worked for years to find balance. Now Sophia, at eight, could recognize patterns and speak truth with compassion.

She was becoming what all schema-informed parents hope to raise: a cycle-breaker[30].

Signs of Schema-Resilient Children

Schema-resilient children don't avoid all wounds—that's impossible. Instead, they develop capacities that prevent wounds from becoming fixed patterns. You'll recognize them by:

Emotional Fluency: They name feelings accurately, express them appropriately, and help others do the same. "I'm frustrated because I expected differently" rather than tantruming or shutting down.

Pattern Recognition: They spot schemas in action—their own, their parents', their peers'. "Is this about what's happening now or something from before?"

Secure Sense of Self: Their worth isn't tied to achievement, others' opinions, or perfect behavior. They know they're lovable as-is.

Boundary Flexibility: They can be close without enmeshment, independent without isolation. Connection and autonomy dance together.

Repair Confidence: They initiate repairs, accept apologies, and trust relationships can handle rupture. Conflict doesn't mean catastrophe.

Growth Orientation: They see mistakes as learning, struggles as development, feelings as information. Life is experiment, not test.

Compassionate Truth-Telling: They speak honestly but kindly, even to authority. "That hurt my feelings" comes as easily as "I love you."

Celebrating Breakthrough Moments

Every schema-informed family has breakthrough moments worth celebrating[31]. Not perfection—breakthroughs. The moments when generational patterns visibly break:

The Abandonment Breakthrough: Your child confidently goes to camp, secure in your love across distance. They miss you without desperation, return joyfully without drama.

The Mistrust Breakthrough: Your teenager tells you about a friendship problem, trusting your response. They navigate relationships with appropriate caution, not paranoia.

The Emotional Deprivation Breakthrough: Your child seeks comfort naturally, offers it freely. Emotions flow in your home like welcome guests, not intruders.

The Defectiveness Breakthrough: Your child admits a mistake without shame spiraling. "I messed up" comes with problem-solving, not self-attack.

The Failure Breakthrough: Your child quits an activity they don't enjoy without identity crisis. They try new things for joy, not achievement.

Document these moments. Write them down, take pictures, create a "breakthrough book." On hard days—and there will be hard days—these reminders show how far you've come.

Preparing Children for Their Own Parenting

The ultimate test of cycle-breaking comes when your children become parents. Are they prepared to recognize their own patterns? Can they heal while parenting? The preparation begins now:

Share the Journey: Age-appropriately discuss your healing work. "I'm learning to worry less because my parents worried too much. Someday you might notice patterns from our family you want to change too."

Normalize Imperfection: "All parents make mistakes. The important part is noticing and repairing."

Teach Meta-Awareness: Help them observe their own patterns. "What do you notice about how you handle frustration?"

Model Ongoing Growth: Show them healing is lifelong. "I'm still learning new things about myself."

Create Family Narratives: Tell stories of growth and healing. "Remember when Grandma learned to say 'I love you'? People can always change."

Build Tool Kits: Ensure they have emotional, relational, and practical tools for their future.

The Ongoing Nature of Healing

Healing isn't a destination—it's a way of traveling[32]. Schema-informed parents learn this through:

Developmental Surprises: New stages reveal hidden patterns. Your healed abandonment issues resurface when your child leaves for college.

Life Stressors: Job loss, illness, moves can reactivate dormant schemas. Old patterns whisper during new challenges.

Intergenerational Encounters: Watching your children parent (babysitting, pets, play) shows both progress and work remaining.

Cultural Shifts: Social media, global events, technological changes create new schema challenges you couldn't anticipate.

The ongoing nature isn't failure—it's reality. Healing happens in spirals, not straight lines. You'll face similar issues at deeper levels, with greater awareness, more tools.

Case Studies: Success Stories Across Different Schemas

Case Study 1: Three Generations Breaking Abandonment
The Chen family represents extraordinary transformation[33]. Grandmother Liu fled war, clinging to children for survival.

Mother Wei rebelled through distance, moving continents away. Daughter Mei felt torn between cultures and attachments.

Through family therapy spanning countries and video calls, they mapped their abandonment legacy. Liu shared war stories never told. Wei grieved the mother she needed but couldn't have. Mei learned her struggles weren't personal but historical.

Now Mei, at 16, speaks three languages: English, Mandarin, and Emotional Fluency. She spent summer with grandmother Liu, no longer triggering abandonment but offering presence. She plans to study abroad—not to escape but to explore, secure in unbreakable bonds across any distance.

Case Study 2: From Mistrust to Community Leadership
Marcus grew up in foster care, developing severe mistrust. His son Jordan absorbed the vigilance despite Marcus's healing efforts. By adolescence, Jordan trusted no one, expected betrayal, isolated completely[34].

The breakthrough came through unexpected avenue: theater. Drama class required vulnerability, ensemble trust, emotional risk. Initially terrified, Jordan discovered safe space to explore connection. The drama teacher, trauma-informed, recognized patterns and supported growth.

Jordan not only learned to trust but became peer mentor for other isolated students. He started support group: "Trust Issues Anonymous," helping classmates navigate friendship. At graduation, Marcus wept watching his son's speech about learning to let people in. The boy who trusted no one had become bridge for others.

Case Study 3: Emotional Availability Across Generations
The Williams family seemed successful externally— achievements, accolades, accumulation. Internally, emotional emptiness spanned generations[35]. Great-grandmother's

depression-era survival required emotional shutdown. Each generation inherited the deprivation differently.

The pattern broke when eight-year-old Jasmine refused inheritance. "Why doesn't anyone in our family cry?" she asked at great-grandmother's funeral. Her question cracked family's emotional permafrost.

What followed: family therapy introducing feeling wheels, emotion charades, vulnerability practices. Great-grandmother, at 89, spoke feelings for first time. Grandmother learned emotional vocabulary at 67. Mother modeled messy feelings at 45. Jasmine, at 8, taught them all.

Now Jasmine, 18, studies psychology, specializing in intergenerational trauma. Her thesis: "How Children Lead Family Emotional Revolution." She interviews families where children catalyzed healing. The emotionally deprived family produced an emotional healer.

Practical Elements

Family Healing Timeline

Create visual representation of your journey:

1. **Past Line**: Mark major schema events in previous generations
2. **Present Line**: Note current healing work and breakthroughs
3. **Future Line**: Envision possibilities for coming generations
4. **Connection Points**: Show how past informs present, present shapes future
5. **Celebration Markers**: Highlight moments patterns broke

Update annually, involving children age-appropriately. Watch the timeline shift from trauma to triumph.

Letters to Your Future Grandchildren

Write letters to grandchildren not yet born:

Dear Future Grandchild,

I'm writing this as I heal patterns passed through our family for generations. By the time you read this, these patterns will be memories, not active wounds. Here's what I want you to know:

Your parent (my child) is learning to love without clinging, trust without naivety, feel without drowning, accept imperfection, define success broadly. If old patterns whisper to you, know that whispers fade with each generation.

You are born into a family that chooses growth...

Seal letters for your children to open when they become parents.

Creating Family Healing Rituals

Develop rituals marking growth:

- **Monthly Pattern Check-ins**: What patterns did we interrupt this month?
- **Seasonal Schema Reviews**: How are we growing with the seasons?
- **Annual Healing Celebrations**: Mark anniversary of beginning the work
- **Breakthrough Ceremonies**: Special recognition for major pattern breaks
- **Story Circles**: Share healing stories across generations

Resource Guide for Continued Growth

Build family library of healing resources:

Books: Age-appropriate options about emotions, relationships, growth *Podcasts*: Family-friendly content about mental health *Apps*: Emotional regulation, mindfulness, communication tools *Community*: List of trusted therapists, support groups, healing friends *Practices*: Family's favorite regulation techniques, repair protocols *Emergency Plans*: What to do when schemas activate strongly

The Generation That Heals

Sophia, now 18, speaks at her high school graduation. She thanks her parents for their courage to heal, making her healing possible. She describes growing up aware of patterns but not controlled by them, supported in growth but not pressured to achieve, loved unconditionally while learning healthy conditions.

"My parents gave me the gift of consciousness," she says. "I know our family patterns. I can see them, name them, choose differently. I am not bound by generational trauma. I am free to create new patterns. And I will."

This is the ripple effect. One parent choosing awareness creates children who expect growth. Those children normalize healing for their peers. Their peers bring questions home. Other families begin journeys. Communities shift. Generations transform.

You won't see all the ripples. Some will extend beyond your lifetime. But every schema you interrupt, every pattern you break, every moment you choose consciousness over compulsion sends waves forward. Your great-great-grandchildren will live differently because you chose to heal.

The cycle-breakers you're raising will face challenges you can't imagine with tools you helped them develop. They'll have their own patterns to notice, their own work to do. But they'll start ahead, building on your foundation, reaching heights you couldn't achieve.

This is how humanity heals—one family, one generation, one conscious moment at a time.

Takeaways:

- **Schema-resilient children** show emotional fluency, pattern recognition, and repair confidence
- **Breakthrough moments** deserve documentation and celebration as evidence of change
- **Preparing children for future parenting** involves transparency about ongoing healing work
- **Healing happens in spirals** with similar issues faced at deeper levels over time
- **Children often catalyze** family healing through innocent questions and observations
- **The ripple effect extends** beyond your family as others witness and begin their own journeys

Conclusion: The Courage to Change

I began this book with a moment of recognition—hearing my mother's voice emerge from my mouth, watching my daughter's face crumble. That moment changed everything, not because it was unique but because it was universal. Every parent has these moments when past and present collide, when we become what we swore we'd never be.

The fifteen chapters between that moment and this one have been a journey through the layers of inherited patterns, the complexity of healing while parenting, the courage required to change generational trajectories. If you've made it this far, you've already shown remarkable bravery. Examining our schemas—those deep patterns that feel like identity itself—requires willingness to be uncomfortable, vulnerable, imperfect.

You Don't Have to Be Fully Healed to Parent Well

Here's what I've learned through my own journey and witnessing hundreds of families transform: Perfect healing isn't the goal[36]. You don't need to be schema-free to raise emotionally healthy children. In fact, your ongoing healing work might be the greatest gift you give them.

Children don't need parents who never struggle. They need parents who struggle consciously. When your child watches you recognize a pattern mid-activation and choose differently, they learn change is possible. When they see you repair after a schema-driven mistake, they learn relationships can handle truth. When they witness your ongoing growth, they learn healing is lifelong, not shameful.

The parents who've touched me most aren't those who've "arrived" but those still traveling. Like Marcus, who after years of mistrust work, told his teenage son, "I'm still learning to trust. Some days are harder than others. But I'm not giving up." His

122

honesty gave his son permission to have his own struggles without shame.

Or Sarah, whose abandonment fears still spike during transitions but who's learned to name them: "My scared parts are acting up because you're growing. That's my work, not yours." Her daughter learned early that she wasn't responsible for managing her mother's emotions—a cycle broken through acknowledgment.

Small Changes Create Generational Impact

The mathematics of generational healing astound me[37]. One moment of choosing awareness over automation affects:

- Your nervous system (immediate)
- Your child's experience (minutes)
- Your relationship dynamic (hours)
- Your family patterns (days)
- Your child's future parenting (decades)
- Your grandchildren's inheritance (generations)

Consider Emma, who caught herself saying, "Big girls don't cry" to her four-year-old. She stopped, knelt down, said instead, "All people cry sometimes. Tears help our feelings move through." That ten-second shift meant:

- Her daughter kept emotional expression
- Tears became acceptable in their home
- Her daughter won't shame her children's tears
- Multiple generations freed from emotional suppression

You don't need grand gestures or perfect execution. Small, repeated choices to interrupt patterns accumulate into transformation[38]. Every schema you notice without acting on, every repair you initiate, every moment of consciousness matters more than you can imagine.

Community Accelerates Healing

The isolation of schema work nearly broke me early on. I thought healing meant solving everything alone—another schema-driven belief. The breakthrough came when I found others on similar journeys. Suddenly, I wasn't the only parent struggling with inherited patterns. My challenges weren't proof of failure but evidence of courage.

Community provides what solo healing cannot:

- **Mirrors**: Others reflect your progress when you can't see it
- **Models**: Watch different approaches to similar patterns
- **Support**: Borrowed strength during difficult passages
- **Celebration**: Witnesses to breakthrough moments
- **Normalization**: Everyone struggles, everyone grows

Whether online or in-person, formal or informal, find your people. Join parenting groups focused on healing. Start conversations about generational patterns. Share this book and discuss it. Create the community you need if it doesn't exist.

Hope for the Future

As I write this conclusion, my daughter—the one who received those sharp words that began this journey—is now a young adult. Last week, she called to process a conflict with her roommate. "I noticed I was getting defensive like we used to in our family," she said. "So I took a break and came back when I could listen."

She's breaking patterns I didn't even know we had. She expects growth from herself and others. She repairs relationships naturally. She feels her feelings without drowning or suppressing. She is living proof that cycles can break, that one generation's courage creates another's freedom.

This is the hope I offer you: Your children can have what you didn't. Not perfect childhoods—those don't exist and wouldn't serve them. But childhoods where:

- Emotions are welcomed guests
- Mistakes become learning
- Love feels secure even through conflict
- Growth is expected and supported
- Patterns are discussed, not hidden

Your grandchildren can inherit emotional wealth instead of emotional poverty. Your great-grandchildren might not even understand what schemas are because they won't need to—you've cleared the patterns that would have bound them.

Final Resources

Professional Help Guide

Seeking therapy isn't failure—it's acceleration. Look for therapists who understand:

- Intergenerational trauma
- Schema therapy approaches
- Attachment theory
- Family systems
- Trauma-informed care

Interview therapists about their approach to generational patterns. Find someone who honors your courage while supporting your growth.

Recommended Reading Progression

Continue your learning journey:

1. *Adult Children of Emotionally Immature Parents* - Lindsay Gibson
2. *The Body Keeps the Score* - Bessel van der Kolk
3. *Parenting from the Inside Out* - Daniel Siegel
4. *Hold Me Tight* - Sue Johnson
5. *Self-Compassion* - Kristin Neff

Online Community Access

Join communities of schema-informed parents:

- Schema Therapy International Society
- Adult Children of Alcoholics/Dysfunctional Families
- Postpartum Support International (trauma-informed)
- Local parenting groups focused on healing

Quick Reference Guides

Keep accessible:

- Schema recognition cheat sheet
- Age-appropriate response guides
- Repair protocol reminders
- Emergency regulation techniques
- Progress celebration trackers

The Courage Continues

The courage to change isn't a one-time decision but a daily practice. Some days you'll respond from schemas despite your best intentions. Some days the patterns will feel stronger than your tools. Some days you'll wonder if the work matters.

On those days, remember: Every parent reading this book is somewhere on the same journey. We're all learning to see patterns we inherited as choices, not destinies. We're all practicing consciousness in the midst of chaos. We're all breaking cycles while building new ones.

Your children are watching you choose growth over stagnation, repair over perfection, consciousness over automation. They're learning that humans can change, that love includes accountability, that families can heal. They're inheriting possibility instead of prison.

The work is hard. The work is holy. The work is worth it.

From my healing family to yours, I offer this blessing: May you find courage in community, strength in vulnerability, and hope in small moments of consciousness. May your children know security you didn't, express emotions you couldn't, and parent from wholeness you're still building.

The cycles stop here. The healing starts now. The generations to come will thank you.

With respect for your courage and hope for our collective healing,

Your companion on the journey

Conclusion Takeaways:

- **Imperfect healing is sufficient** - consciousness matters more than completion
- **Small moments accumulate** into generational transformation
- **Community support** accelerates and sustains the healing journey
- **Hope lives in daily choices** to interrupt patterns and choose growth
- **Professional help** represents wisdom, not weakness

- **The courage to change** is a daily practice, not a one-time decision

Companion Resources

Sarah stared at her completed schema assessment, numbers swimming before her eyes. She'd identified with nearly every abandonment statement, scoring fours and fives across the board. The knowledge felt heavy—seeing her patterns laid bare in black and white. But then she flipped to the emergency response card, reading the simple words: "This feeling is temporary. Your child is safe. You are safe. Breathe."

These companion resources exist because awareness without tools is overwhelming. You need more than understanding—you need practical, grab-them-in-the-moment supports for when schemas activate and your hard-won knowledge evaporates in the heat of triggered responses. Think of these resources as your schema first-aid kit, always within reach when patterns threaten to take over.

Digital Components

The digital age offers something previous generations of parents lacked—immediate access to support in triggering moments. Your smartphone becomes a healing tool, connecting you to resources exactly when schemas spike.

1. Schema Assessment Tool (Parent & Child Versions)

The parent assessment goes beyond simple questionnaires[39]. This interactive tool adapts based on your responses, diving deeper into patterns that score high. You'll receive:

- **Personalized schema profile** showing your unique combination
- **Trigger prediction** based on your pattern intersections
- **Custom intervention suggestions** for your specific schemas
- **Progress tracking** to see changes over time

The child version uses age-appropriate language and engaging graphics. Rather than clinical terms, children identify with characters representing different patterns. "Sometimes I feel like Worried Owl" becomes a way for children to communicate their emotional experience without pathologizing labels.

Case Example: Jennifer took the assessment monthly for a year. Watching her abandonment scores decrease from 4.8 to 3.2 provided concrete evidence of her healing. More importantly, her children's assessments showed decreasing anxiety scores—proof the cycle was breaking.

2. Downloadable Worksheets and Exercises

Over forty worksheets transform book concepts into daily practice[40]. Each worksheet includes:

- **Clear instructions** for independent use
- **Examples** showing completed versions
- **Modification suggestions** for different ages
- **Integration tips** for family use

Popular worksheets include:

- Daily Schema Check-In (morning awareness practice)
- Trigger Tracking Log (pattern identification)
- Repair Planning Template (post-activation recovery)
- Family Pattern Mapping (visual representation)
- Progress Celebration Tracker (acknowledging growth)

These aren't academic exercises but practical tools. The "Schema Storm Preparation" worksheet helped the Chen family plan responses before visiting triggering relatives. Having strategies written down meant less reactive parenting, more conscious choices.

3. Video Demonstrations of Co-Regulation Techniques

Reading about co-regulation differs from seeing it. The video library shows real parents (with permission) managing triggered moments. You'll see:

- **Body positioning** that promotes calm
- **Voice tone** shifts that soothe
- **Breathing techniques** demonstrated
- **Touch approaches** for different ages
- **Recovery sequences** after ruptures

Each video includes multiple examples because co-regulation isn't one-size-fits-all. Watch how different parents manage similar triggers, finding approaches that match your family's style.

Case Example: Marcus couldn't grasp co-regulation from reading. Watching a father help his panicking child through separation anxiety—seeing the breath matching, the lowered voice, the patient presence—gave him a template. He practiced with the video, then with his son. "I could copy what I saw until it became natural," he reported.

4. Private Online Community Access

The isolation of schema work breaks when you find others on the same journey[41]. This moderated community provides:

- **24/7 peer support** for triggered moments
- **Success story sharing** for hope building
- **Challenge processing** without judgment
- **Resource exchanges** between members
- **Expert guidance** during weekly moderator hours

Community guidelines ensure safety: no advice-giving, no schema shaming, no comparison competing. Just witnessed experiences and mutual support.

The community saved Lisa during a particularly difficult night. Her daughter's independence assertion triggered every abandonment fear. At 2 AM, she posted her panic. Within minutes, three parents responded—not with solutions but with "I've been there" solidarity. The schema storm passed with witnesses.

5. Monthly Q&A Sessions with Author

Live sessions address real-time challenges. Submit questions beforehand or ask live. Topics rotate through:

- **Developmental challenges** and schema adaptation
- **Partner conflicts** around different patterns
- **Extended family** navigation strategies
- **Breakthrough celebrations** and community wins
- **Resource recommendations** for specific situations

Sessions are recorded for those who can't attend live, building a searchable library of practical wisdom.

Quick Reference Guides

Knowledge evaporates during schema activation. These guides provide instant access to crucial information when triggered minds can't access complex concepts.

1. Schema Trigger Emergency Cards

Wallet-sized cards for each schema containing:

- **Recognition signs**: "You're activated when..."
- **Grounding statement**: Schema-specific affirmation
- **Three-breath pause**: Visual breathing guide
- **Simple action**: One thing to do right now
- **Repair reminder**: "Come back when calm"

Abandonment Card Example:

- Triggered when: Child chooses others/space
- Truth: Love survives distance
- Action: Name the feeling, don't fix
- Breathe: In-2-3-4, Out-2-3-4
- Later: Share your growth with child

Parents report keeping cards everywhere—wallet, car, kitchen drawer. "It's like having a therapist in my pocket," one mother explained.

2. Age-Appropriate Response Guides

Development changes everything. These guides provide schema-informed responses by age:

Toddler (2-3) Mistrust Response:

- They need: Safety through predictability
- You say: "Mommy keeps you safe"
- You do: Maintain calm presence
- Avoid: Interrogation or panic

Teen (14-17) Abandonment Response:

- They need: Independence with connection
- You say: "I love you and trust you"
- You do: Offer without requiring
- Avoid: Clinging or pursuing

Each age includes five schema-specific guides, laminated for durability.

3. Co-Regulation Technique Library

Beyond videos, this illustrated guide shows:

- **Body positions** for different scenarios
- **Voice modulation** techniques
- **Touch guidelines** by age and preference
- **Environmental modifications** for calm
- **Recovery sequences** post-activation

Visual learners particularly appreciate seeing techniques drawn out. One father posted his guide on the refrigerator, making co-regulation a family practice.

4. Partner Communication Templates

Schema conflicts between partners need specific language[42]. Templates include:

When Partner's Schema Triggers Yours: "I notice my [schema] is activated by your [behavior]. Can we pause and reconnect?"

Planning Unified Response: "Our child needs [developmental need]. How can we meet that despite our different schemas?"

Repair After Schema Clash: "I reacted from my [schema], not from wisdom. Can we try again?"

These templates prevent schema battles from becoming relationship wars.

5. Extended Family Scripts

Prepared responses for predictable situations:

Boundary Setting: "We're trying a different approach with our kids. We'd appreciate your support even if you disagree."

Real-Time Intervention: "Mom, let's give Sarah space to feel her feelings. She's learning it's okay to be upset."

Post-Visit Debrief: "Grandma loves you and shows it differently than we do. What felt good about the visit? What felt hard?"

Having scripts ready prevents reactive responses to extended family triggers.

Workbook Elements Throughout

The companion workbook transforms passive reading into active healing[43]. With over forty exercises, fifteen assessment tools, and twenty-five real-world scripts, it becomes your practical healing guide.

40+ Practical Exercises

Exercises build systematically:

1. **Awareness Building** (Exercises 1-10): Recognizing patterns
2. **Skill Development** (Exercises 11-25): Learning new responses
3. **Integration Practice** (Exercises 26-35): Applying with family
4. **Advanced Healing** (Exercises 36-40+): Deeper work

Each exercise includes:

- Purpose statement
- Materials needed
- Step-by-step instructions
- Troubleshooting tips
- Integration suggestions

Popular Exercise: The Schema Family Tree Map patterns through generations using colors and symbols. Children love participating, choosing colors for different feelings. One family framed their completed tree, marking healing progress with gold stars.

15+ Assessment Tools

Beyond initial schema identification:

- **Daily Trigger Tracker**: Identify pattern frequencies
- **Relationship Schema Map**: See how schemas interact
- **Child Development Checklist**: Schema-informed milestones
- **Progress Measurement Scale**: Track healing markers
- **Family Climate Assessment**: Overall pattern health

Regular assessment reveals subtle progress. The Johnson family's monthly scores showed steady improvement invisible in daily life—evidence that kept them motivated during difficult patches.

25+ Real-World Scripts

Scripts cover common scenarios:

Morning Rush Abandonment Trigger: "I notice I'm getting anxious about you being ready. That's my stuff. Take your time—we'll figure it out together."

Homework Failure Schema: "This is challenging. What part would you like help with? Remember, learning is more important than perfect answers."

Bedtime Emotional Deprivation: "Tell me about your day's feelings. I'm here to listen, not fix."

Parents practice scripts during calm moments, building muscle memory for triggered times.

Family Activity Suggestions

Activities make healing playful:

- **Schema Charades**: Act out patterns safely
- **Feeling Faces Photo Album**: Build emotional vocabulary
- **Pattern Interruption Dance**: Silly movement when triggered
- **Repair Ritual Crafts**: Create family repair symbols
- **Growth Garden**: Plant seeds representing changes

The Martinez family's "Schema Superhero" game helped their children see pattern interruption as powerful. Each family member created a superhero identity opposing their schema—Captain Connection battled Abandonment Villain through the power of secure hugs.

Progress Tracking Templates

What gets measured gets celebrated:

- **Weekly Win Tracker**: Document pattern interruptions
- **Monthly Family Meeting Template**: Structure growth discussions
- **Quarterly Review Guide**: See bigger picture progress
- **Annual Healing Timeline**: Mark major breakthroughs
- **Generational Change Chart**: Track cycle-breaking evidence

Visual progress combats discouragement. The Chen family's chart showed fifty-three successful schema interruptions in one month—invisible victories made visible.

Implementation Strategies

Having resources means nothing without implementation. Start small:

1. **Choose one digital tool** to explore this week
2. **Print one emergency card** for your primary schema
3. **Try one worksheet** with your family
4. **Practice one script** in the mirror
5. **Track one pattern** for seven days

Build slowly. The Patel family spent three months just using emergency cards before adding other tools. "We needed to master basics before advancing," they explained. Now they use multiple resources daily, but the foundation came through patient practice.

Living Implementation

These resources aren't academic exercises but living tools. Sarah, who began this section staring at her abandonment scores, now keeps her emergency card taped inside kitchen cabinets. When her children ask for independence and her chest tightens, she opens a cabinet for water and sees: "Love survives distance."

Her daily schema check-in takes two minutes each morning. The family pattern map hangs in their hallway—not hidden but celebrated as their growth edge. Her children know the co-regulation positions, requesting "butterfly breathing" when upset. The worksheets fill a binder documenting their journey from unconscious patterns to conscious choices.

This is how cycles break—not through perfection but through practical tools used imperfectly but consistently. Every emergency card consulted, every script practiced, every exercise completed weakens schemas' hold on your family's future.

Your Resource Journey Begins

You don't need every resource immediately. Like schema healing itself, resource use develops over time. Start with what calls to you:

- If you're visual, begin with videos
- If you need community, join online first
- If you like structure, worksheets await
- If you need immediate help, print emergency cards
- If you learn through doing, activities beckon

The resources exist to support, not overwhelm. Use what helps, modify what doesn't fit, create new tools as needed. Other families share their innovations in the online community—schema healing is collaborative creation.

One year from now, you'll have your own collection of worn worksheets, modified scripts, personalized tools. You'll know which resources support you in different moments. Your children will request favorite activities, reference family tools naturally, see healing work as normal family life[44].

The companion resources transform this book from information to transformation. They bridge the gap between understanding schemas and interrupting them, between knowing better and doing better, between inherited patterns and chosen responses.

Your healing toolkit awaits. Pick up one tool today. Your future family will thank you[45].

Key Takeaways

- **Digital tools provide 24/7 support** when schemas activate outside therapy hours
- **Emergency cards offer instant grounding** when triggered minds can't access complex concepts
- **Video demonstrations make abstract concepts** concrete and learnable

- **Community connection breaks isolation** inherent in schema healing work
- **Practical exercises transform understanding** into daily family practice
- **Progress tracking provides hope** during difficult phases by showing invisible growth
- **Implementation should be gradual** to avoid overwhelm and ensure sustainable change

Reference

1. Bowlby, J. (1988). A Secure Base: Parent-Child Attachment and Healthy Human Development. Basic Books.
2. Ainsworth, M. D. S., Blehar, M. C., Waters, E., & Wall, S. (1978). Patterns of attachment: A psychological study of the strange situation. Lawrence Erlbaum.
3. Young, J. E., Klosko, J. S., & Weishaar, M. E. (2003). Schema therapy: A practitioner's guide. Guilford Press.
4. Johnson, S. (2019). Attachment theory in practice: Emotionally focused therapy (EFT) with individuals, couples, and families. Guilford Press.
5. van der Kolk, B. (2014). The Body Keeps the Score: Brain, Mind, and Body in the Healing of Trauma. Viking.
6. National Scientific Council on the Developing Child. (2010). Early experiences can alter gene expression and affect long-term development: Working paper no. 10.
7. Shapiro, F. (2001). Eye Movement Desensitization and Reprocessing (EMDR): Basic Principles, Protocols, and Procedures. Guilford Press.
8. Webb, J. (2012). Running on Empty: Overcome Your Childhood Emotional Neglect. Morgan James Publishing.
9. Siegel, D. J. (2012). The Developing Mind: How Relationships and the Brain Interact to Shape Who We Are. Guilford Press.
10. Greenberg, L. S. (2015). Emotion-Focused Therapy: Coaching Clients to Work Through Their Feelings. American Psychological Association.
11. Brown, B. (2012). Daring Greatly: How the Courage to Be Vulnerable Transforms the Way We Live, Love, Parent, and Lead. Gotham Books.
12. Schore, A. N. (2003). Affect Dysregulation and Disorders of the Self. W. W. Norton & Company.

13. Hewitt, P. L., & Flett, G. L. (1991). Perfectionism in the self and social contexts. Journal of Personality and Social Psychology, 60(3), 456-470.
14. Brown, B. (2006). Shame Resilience Theory: A grounded theory study on women and shame. Families in Society, 87(1), 43-52.
15. Winnicott, D. W. (1971). Playing and Reality. Tavistock Publications.
16. Neff, K. (2011). Self-Compassion: The Proven Power of Being Kind to Yourself. William Morrow.
17. Luthar, S. S., & Becker, B. E. (2002). Privileged but pressured? A study of affluent youth. Child Development, 73(5), 1593-1610.
18. Leonard, N. R., Gwadz, M. V., Ritchie, A., Linick, J. L., Cleland, C. M., Elliott, L., & Grethel, M. (2015). A multi-method exploratory study of stress, coping, and substance use among high school youth in private schools. Frontiers in Psychology, 6, 1028.
19. Deci, E. L., & Ryan, R. M. (2000). The "what" and "why" of goal pursuits: Human needs and the self-determination of behavior. Psychological Inquiry, 11(4), 227-268.
20. Dweck, C. (2006). Mindset: The New Psychology of Success. Random House.
21. Siegel, D. J., & Hartzell, M. (2003). Parenting from the Inside Out: How a Deeper Self-Understanding Can Help You Raise Children Who Thrive. Tarcher/Penguin.
22. Balanced Parenting Institute. (2023). The Lighthouse Parenting Model: Research and Practice. Family Education Quarterly, 45(3), 234-251.
23. Powell, B., Cooper, G., Hoffman, K., & Marvin, B. (2013). The Circle of Security Intervention: Enhancing Attachment in Early Parent-Child Relationships. Guilford Press.
24. Young, J. E., & Klosko, J. S. (2019). Schema dynamics in couples: Understanding and treating relationship patterns. Journal of Schema Therapy, 8(2), 45-62.

25. Arntz, A., & Jacob, G. (2013). Schema therapy in practice: An introductory guide to the schema mode approach. Wiley-Blackwell.
26. Loose, C., Graaf, P., & Zarbock, G. (Eds.). (2013). Schema therapy for children and adolescents: A practitioner's guide. Pavilion Publishing.
27. Stallard, P. (2007). Early maladaptive schemas in children: Development and validation of the Schema Inventory for Children. Pavilion Publishing.
28. Rijkeboer, M. M., & de Boo, G. M. (2010). Early maladaptive schemas in children: Development and validation of the Schema Inventory for Children. Pavilion Publishing.
29. Young, J. E., & Brown, G. (2005). Young Schema Questionnaire for Adolescents. Pavilion Publishing.
30. Cori, J. L. (2010). The Emotionally Absent Mother: How to Recognize and Heal the Invisible Effects of Childhood Emotional Neglect. The Experiment.
31. Louis, J. P., Wood, A. M., & Lockwood, G. (2018). Psychometric validation of the Young Parenting Inventory - Revised. PLOS ONE, 13(11), e0205605.
32. Sundag, J., Ascone, L., de Matos Pinto, A., & Lincoln, T. M. (2016). Elucidating the role of Early Maladaptive Schemas for psychotic symptomatology. Psychiatry Research, 238, 53-59.
33. Calvete, E., Orue, I., & Hankin, B. L. (2013). Early maladaptive schemas and social anxiety in adolescents: The mediating role of anxious automatic thoughts. Journal of Anxiety Disorders, 27(3), 278-288.
34. Roelofs, J., Lee, C., Ruijten, T., & Lobbestael, J. (2011). The mediating role of early maladaptive schemas in the relation between quality of attachment relationships and symptoms of depression in adolescents. Behavioural and Cognitive Psychotherapy, 39(4), 471-479.
35. Zeynel, Z., & Uzer, T. (2020). Adverse childhood experiences lead to trans-generational transmission of

early maladaptive schemas. Child Abuse & Neglect, 99, 104235.

36. Kovács, L. N., Takacs, Z. K., Tóth, Z., Simon, E., Schmelowszky, Á., & Kökönyei, G. (2020). Rumination in major depressive and bipolar disorder – a meta-analysis. Journal of Affective Disorders, 276, 1131-1141.

37. Belsky, J., Conger, R., & Capaldi, D. M. (2009). The intergenerational transmission of parenting: Introduction to the special section. Developmental Psychology, 45(5), 1201-1204.

38. Bridgett, D. J., Burt, N. M., Edwards, E. S., & Deater-Deckard, K. (2015). Intergenerational transmission of self-regulation: A multidisciplinary review and integrative conceptual framework. Psychological Bulletin, 141(3), 602-654.

39. Young, J. E., & Brown, G. (2003). Young Schema Questionnaire – Long Form 3 (YSQ-L3). Schema Therapy Institute.

40. Farrell, J. M., & Shaw, I. A. (2012). Group Schema Therapy for Borderline Personality Disorder: A Step-by-Step Treatment Manual with Patient Workbook. Wiley-Blackwell.

41. McKay, M., Wood, J. C., & Brantley, J. (2007). The Dialectical Behavior Therapy Skills Workbook. New Harbinger Publications.

42. Johnson, S. M., & Sanderfer, K. (2016). Created for Connection: The "Hold Me Tight" Guide for Christian Couples. Little, Brown Spark.

43. Kennerley, H. (2014). Overcoming Childhood Trauma: A Self-Help Guide Using Cognitive Behavioral Techniques. Robinson.

44. Roediger, E., Stevens, B. A., & Brockman, R. (2018). Contextual Schema Therapy: An Integrative Approach to Personality Disorders, Emotional Dysregulation, and Interpersonal Functioning. Context Press.

45. Lockwood, G., & Perris, P. (2012). A new look at core emotional needs. In M. van Vreeswijk, J. Broersen, & M. Nadort (Eds.), The Wiley-Blackwell Handbook of Schema Therapy (pp. 41-66). Wiley-Blackwell.

www.ingramcontent.com/pod-product-compliance
Lightning Source LLC
Chambersburg PA
CBHW052011090426
42741CB00008B/1645